WHAT JESUS SAID
about...

> Though this book is designed for group study, it is also intended for your personal enjoyment and spiritual growth. A leader's guide is available from your local bookstore or from your publisher.

Copyright 1989
Beacon Hill Press of Kansas City
Kansas City, Missouri

Printed in the United States of America

ISBN: 083-411-1713

Editor
Stephen M. Miller

Editorial Assistant
Kathryn Roblee

Editorial Committee
Jack Mottweiler, *Chairman*
David Keith
Stephen M. Miller
Carl Pierce
Gene Van Note
Lyle Williams

Photo and Art Credits

Bible Credits

Contents

Chapter 1

...Worry

by Robert M. Holmes

Background Scripture: Psalm 23; Matthew 6:25-34

I HAVE A FRIEND who once expressed two fears. One fear was that if he did not slow down, he could have a heart attack. The other fear was that if he didn't hurry up, he would not be able to accomplish enough before he had his heart attack.

I'm told that Americans consume 97 percent of the world's aspirin. Heart attacks and peptic ulcers are hitting more people, and sooner, than ever before. A lot of folks have ulcers already, and many more may be on their way to having them. But as far as we can tell, Jesus never had them. And as followers of His, perhaps we'd better pause long enough to ask why.

I've heard several explanations. Some say He never lived long enough to get them. One person said He didn't have six children and an ailing wife. Another person explains that He didn't have to repay the national debt or keep drug pushers out of the neighborhood. It's true that Jesus lived in a time that was quite different from ours. The pace was not as fast nor the competition as keen, perhaps. People did not strive for more; they settled for less. Without newscasts every hour, they weren't encumbered with the world's problems in addition to their own. Life was relatively simple and the life span relatively short.

In other words, there were not as many ulcer producers in that ancient Palestinian culture as there are today. But do not underestimate the tensions that surrounded Jesus. He didn't retire from carpentering on a pension. He noted that birds have nests and foxes have holes but the Son of Man had no place to lay His head. He often had no guarantees about the next meal or the next night's lodging. Moreover, He was trying to fulfill an impossible assignment—to bring in a kingdom, or at least start a movement, without benefit of clergy or army or political pull. In fact, He was pretty promptly identified as being in quite a separate camp from clergy, army, or government. And underlying all of this was the prospect of an early end to His earthly life.

In spite of the differences between His culture and ours, Jesus of Nazareth knew pressures that you and I have never known. Yet He never seemed to worry. Why? The answer does not lie in anything that was unique about His physiological makeup or any advantage He may have had that we do not have. The answer lies, rather, in resources available to all of us of which Jesus was willing to take advantage.

Secret I

To begin with, Jesus never lost His perspective about himself, His work, where He fit into things, and what did and did not depend on Him. To gain a proper perspective, whether it be of a painting or of your lifework, you must stand back for a time and set yourself apart in order to get a broader, fuller look. Jesus had to retreat time and again, and we must do the same.

The real purpose of a retreat is not just to "get away from it all" but to get a better view. It's not so much like hiding in a cave, where you can see nothing, as it is climbing a mountain, where you can see the entire landscape, where you can ask, How is everything fitting together and where am I fitting into the scheme? This is where a contemplative monk, cloistered in his monastery, may miss the force of Jesus' message. It is not hard to retreat from a world of struggle and conflict. It's a cinch to find peace of mind when you are divorced from the world. The challenge lies in keeping peace of mind when you are *in* the world.

The purpose of the retreats you and I experience periodically (vacations, "nights out," long weekends, a walk in the park, "spiritual renewal weekends," etc.) is to help us regain perspective, to see ourselves more properly in relation to the world around us and to God, and to recharge our spiritual batteries with power to meet the challenges that lie around us.

It is easy to get obsessed with our indispensability. I've known some busy mothers who have had the liberating experience of having to go to the hospital for a few days and later discovering that the family got along just fine. The family need not foster a dependency but can be a partnership. This can be an important discovery for the entire family. Or your experience may be more like mine. When you come back to your own job after having been gone awhile, you may find you really haven't been missed, and that things have run quite smoothly without you. We all need to learn, occasionally, that we have a valuable contribution to make but that the world does not rest on our shoulders.

Getting away sometimes helps us see problems in their proper perspective. Many years ago a certain newspaper carried at the top of its editorial column these lines:

> Some of your hurts you have cured,
> And the sharpest you still have survived;
> But what torments of grief you've endured
> From the evils that never arrived.

Jesus said simply, "Do not be anxious about tomorrow, for tomorrow will be anxious for itself. Let the day's own trouble be sufficient for the day" (Matthew 6:34, RSV). This much of Jesus' formula for avoiding ulcers is nothing new to us. But how do you just relax in the midst of deadlines, keen competition, heavy schedules, and frightening world problems?

Secret 2

The second secret for avoiding ulcers is not as obvious as the first. Jesus was not afraid to fail. And you know, I think most of us are. Success has become a byword in our culture. Everyone must succeed. Graduating classes even try to predict who is most likely to do so. Recent tests among college students indicate that more than half of them put financial success as their number one goal in life.

Jesus, on the other hand, seemed not at all concerned about being a "success." During the 40-day interval in the wilderness after His baptism, He tried to get a careful understanding of His mission in life, and He rejected three specific forms of success—fame, wealth, and power. From that time on He refused to be dismayed by people's disappointment in Him. First the hierarchy scoffed; then John the Baptist became disillusioned; His own family questioned His choices; and finally even His disciples grew skeptical.

Jesus was considered a failure by nearly everyone on earth whose opinion meant a lot to Him.

Apparently Jesus never lost any sleep over this, though many of us would have. There is practically nothing we would rather avoid than to be considered a failure in the eyes of our fellow human beings—professionally, financially, or socially. I suspect more ulcers are generated by the single human drive for success than by any other cause. This drive can fool us. We are a good deal more concerned about keeping up with the Joneses than we think we are. We want to provide for our families—for their sakes, of course, and we don't want to do a less adequate job of it than the Joneses do. What the economist Thorstein Veblen long ago called "conspicuous consumption" is a means of showing the world—particularly the Joneses—just how successful we really are.

Parental problems, more often than not, involve the fear of what others will think. Concern about my teenager and the places he goes, or concern about my four-year-old who hasn't stopped sucking his thumb, or my toddler who expresses his anger in public, is complicated by my more unconscious concern for what people will think of me as a parent.

Well, Jones never bothered Jesus. At no time did Jesus ever define His course of action on the basis of what people expected of Him, and He tried to free us from this worry as well. It is God's expectation that counts.

Jesus said that if you labor in trust, God will see to your basic needs; but don't be anxious about your life, what you shall eat, what you shall put on. Life is a whole lot more than that! We may not get rich, we may not become famous, we may not gain power; but life is more than that, and if we live in trust, God will provide us with all that is required for a full and meaningful life.

There is an art to failing successfully, it seems to me.

A homemaker may have to choose between being a meticulous housekeeper, or even an award-winning church worker, and being a good parent. A provider may have to choose between earning extra money outside the home and being present more often with the family. I have known some people who, looking back, wished they had settled for a cheaper *house* in order to have a more joyous *home*. A minister, a teacher, a person in public service, and many others whose work, like an iceberg, is largely unseen, constantly face the choice between doing what needs to be done and doing what will look good to onlookers. They also must make choices among many good projects that cannot all be completed in the time available. One cannot save the entire world before the children get home from school.

Jesus was the most conscientious person who ever lived, but He was not, thank God, a perfectionist. In fact, it's remarkable how disorganized His efforts appear to have been. As far as establishing a movement was concerned, or starting a revolution, He didn't organize anything. He just went on from day to day, loving and serving, and listening. The perfection of His life was in His love, and nothing else. This is the perfection toward which we are called to strive, with the assurance that repentance for failure to love well enough brings, with forgiveness, a power to love better. We have every reason to seek this kind of perfection (or, as Jesus put it, to "seek first his kingdom and his righteousness," Matthew 6:33). But if, in anything else, you are a perfectionist, you may be on your way to an ulcer—something Jesus never had.

Secret 3

One more reason Jesus never had an ulcer: He never forgot who was in charge. He refused to shoulder more responsibility than was properly His. This is one of our most common mistakes. It has been well said that one of the finest arts of the religious life is "letting go and letting God." At this art Jesus was indeed a master. He seemed to know the meaning of Reinhold Niebuhr's famous "Prayer for Serenity."

O God, grant us the serenity to accept
What cannot be changed;
The courage to change what can be changed,
And the wisdom to know the one from the other.

Jesus never forgot who was in charge. He bore un-
measured burdens, He faced extreme temptations, He confronted insurmountable obstacles, He was mercilessly
treated, but He never forgot who was in charge.

Peace of mind is more than just relaxing. Jesus didn't
say, "Forget it, it will all turn out." But He did teach that God
will order the future as God has done the past, and that God
is on the side of the values that count the most.

Whoever knows this God of supreme power and perfect
love and ultimate victory is not just likely to avoid ulcers but
is certain to find abundant life.

Chapter 2

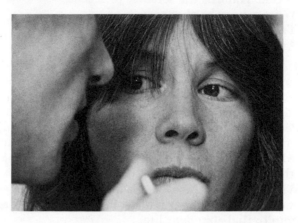

... Temptation

by Lloyd John Ogilvie

Background Scripture: Psalm 66:10-12; Luke 11:4; 1 Corinthians 10:13; James 1:2-3, 12-15

OVER BRUNCH one Sunday after church, a conversation with my friend Bob suddenly shifted from general pleasantries to a profound discussion that lasted late into the afternoon. The Lord's Prayer was on Bob's mind, and he wanted to talk about it.

"I've repeated the Lord's Prayer ever since I was a little boy," Bob said thoughtfully. "This morning in the worship service as we prayed it together, I found it difficult to say the words, 'Lead us not into temptation.' Lately I've been thinking a lot about that. I can't imagine that God would ever deliberately lead me into temptation. So why pray that He won't?

"Frankly," Bob went on, "I've got enough temptations to battle with as it is. The idea that God might lead me into more and that I have to beg Him not to with this line from the Lord's Prayer really has me confused. I guess I've missed the point. But whatever the answer is—I'm not going to pray that part of the Lord's Prayer again until I'm sure."

A Popular Answer

How would you respond to Bob? In a surface interpretation, many of us would suggest a popular understanding of the petition. We'd tell Bob that it really means "Keep us from temptation and subdue the evil one who constantly tries to lure us into temptation."

And we'd be right—at least for openers. We're tempted all the time, and we need the Lord to protect us from evil influence. We are really asking that He intervene to keep us out of relationships with people who would lead us astray and out of situations in which our faith might be compromised.

To fortify our interpretation of Jesus' hard saying, we might underline some biblical cross-references that have become a source of courage for us in our battles with temptation. We'd probably turn to James 1:13 as a strong reaffirmation that God does not tempt us. "When tempted, no one should say, 'God is tempting me.' For God cannot be tempted by evil, nor does he tempt anyone."

And when we've been under the pressure of some temptation, we've felt a special surge of strength from Paul's reassurance of God's faithfulness. "No temptation has seized you except what is common to man. And God is faithful; he will not let you be tempted beyond what you can bear. But when you are tempted, he will also provide a way out so that you can stand up under it" (1 Corinthians 10:13).

All of us could give specific examples from our own lives of how God has blocked us from pressing on with some selfish desire that would hurt us or someone else. Who could make it through any week—any day for that matter—without the ways of escape that He provides to keep us from saying or doing what might destroy us?

God makes us uncomfortable with "white lies" that may become a pattern of dishonesty. Before we step over the line and damage or destroy someone's character, He confronts us with our demeaning attitudes and cutting words of gossip. When we titillate our sexual needs by flirtation that could lead to sexual sins, He blocks us before we go too far. And think of the many times when He has made it impossible to go ahead with unguided decisions that would have led us away from Him and His plans for us.

Thank God that in His infinite wisdom and direct involvement in our lives He does close doors, put up roadblocks, and actively hinder us from doing what is not His best for us. And what's more, when we do fail, the Lord helps us deal with the temptation to condemn ourselves. The evil one lurks waiting for those times. The one thing he tries to keep us from doing is confessing our failure, receiving forgiveness, and making a new beginning. But Christ our Savior and Friend is more powerful than Satan. He gives us strength to overcome the temptation to become immobilized with self-condemnation.

So, on the basis of this first level of understanding, we pray, "Lord, You know how weak I am at times, and how beguiling the evil one continues to be. Keep me out of the clutches of temptation!" That's a needed daily prayer, and our Lord answers in wondrous ways beyond our deserving or expectation. But that's not all Jesus intended in this hard saying.

Moving Deeper

We move out into deeper water when we understand that the Greek word for "temptation" in this petition can also be translated as "trial." So in this context, the petition could be worded, "Lead us not into trial, but keep us from the evil one."

We've all known our share of trying times. They occur when our patience, strength, or endurance is stretched to the breaking point. People disappoint us, sickness invades our life, grief over the loss of loved ones engulfs us, or suddenly a reversal dashes our hopes and dreams.

Once again, we can't imagine that our loving Father would intentionally send trying times like these. We hold tenaciously onto our conviction that He does not send difficulties. Rather, we bring many of our problems on ourselves. Other problems may come from the people around us. And Satan always has his arsenal loaded with diabolical ammunition of suffering. No, we say, God does not lead us into trials; but He may use them to help us grow as people.

At this point in our discussion over brunch, my friend Bob expressed appreciation for the reassurance of my explanation of how God helps us in both temptations and trials. "But," he interjected, "you still have not dealt with that confusing 'lead us not' aspect of the petition." Then I told Bob I had kept that as a part of the big plunge into the deep.

The Big Plunge

The words "lead us not" really mean "bring us not." Any authentic explanation of what this petition means must include that idea. The Lord can and will bring us into whatever He considers necessary to keep us open and receptive to Him as Lord of our lives.

A test is whatever exposes the real nature of something. In the laboratory we test a substance to determine its component parts. Metals are tested for their strength and durability. A car is road-tested to evaluate its safety.

I believe God tests us, not because He wants to expose our weaknesses but to introduce us to our real selves. The test is for us, not for Him.

Think of it this way. When we drift from the Lord and begin to run our own lives and resist the nudges and urging of His Spirit, we are on a collision course with disaster. But graciously, He steps into the path of our speeding lives to stop us. So, the test is whatever means He uses to wake us up to where we are heading—to expose us to our real destination—before it's too late. When we seek independence from accountability to Him, something has to be done.

Sometimes the Lord may test us by using the tragedies that happen in our lives to alert us to how far we have wandered from Him. Sickness and pain can be megaphone warnings from Him. The dark night of the soul can make us long again for the dawn of His love.

This hard saying, "Do not bring us to the test," is really a daily vaccination to prevent the necessity for God's having to test us.

Now we are ready for the hardest question of all. Would it be love to allow us to drift until we no longer sense our need or desire for the Lord? Hardly.

When I think of how God does put us to the test before it's too late, Jerry also comes to mind. I had known Jerry during his seminary days here in the Los Angeles area. Of all the seminarians I have known, few had shown more promise than Jerry. After seminary, he became the pastor of a church in the Midwest. He threw himself into the duties of building up the membership, starting a building program, and working with people night and day. Soon his quiet time each day with the Lord was set aside to meet his busy schedule. Eventually, he hardly prayed at all, except as a part of his public pastoral duties. He did Bible study only to get ready to preach, seldom for the enrichment of his own spiritual life.

Then about four years or so into his ministry, Jerry began to act strangely. He became autocratic, hostile, and angry. Soon his marriage was in trouble. The officers of his church warned him that his attitude was crippling his ministry. The forward movement of the church ground to a halt. Jerry blamed the resistance of his people. One day, he left.

Jerry had had it with the ministry. Not knowing where he was headed, he got into his car and began driving west. Three weeks later, Jerry arrived in Los Angeles. The lonely drive over the mountains and down to the coast had been a traumatic experience. But the Lord had been with him and confronted him with his four-year drift from Him. By the time he reached me, he was ready to take a long, hard look at himself.

Fortunately, Jerry didn't try to put the blame on his wife, the difficult religious traditionalists in his church, or the demands of his schedule. He realized that he had tried to live on his own strength and talents rather than on God's power. And whether or not he ever had a chance to serve as a clergyman again, he wanted the joy and peace he'd known before he had closed God out of his life.

After several visits, Jerry was ready to go home and face whatever happened. The Lord stepped in to pull off a miracle. Both his wife and his church welcomed Jerry back. He now sees that only God could have made that possible. This is what he wrote me.

I'm sure the Lord has been trying to get through to me for a long time. He didn't have to wait until I almost lost my family and my church. It was I who held Him at arm's length. The near nervous breakdown I went through was not His doing, but my own. The wonder of it all is that He didn't let me crash completely. He let the boil fester until it came to a head, and then He lanced it with His judgment and healed it with His grace. My great regret is that I fought against His healing for so long. Now I pray constantly that I'll not make that kind of a heartbreaking encounter with the Lord necessary again.

Unfortunately, I also remember people whose lives have fallen apart and who even then have resisted the Lord's help. "What did I do to deserve this?" they wonder, rather than asking, "What is the Lord seeking to tell me in this?" The Lord's efforts to reach them in their difficulties are rebuffed. Bitterness sets in, and God is made the enemy.

A Victorious Prayer

With our new understanding of this hard saying of Jesus we can honestly say, "Lord, help me to live in such close communion with You, open to Your guidance and willing to obey, that You do not have to bring me to the test of my love for You. Thank You for rescuing me from Satan's power and from his beguiling influence."

What I've written in this chapter is essentially what I shared with my friend Bob that Sunday afternoon during and after brunch. Bob sat silently for a long time after our discussion. Then he spoke with intensity.

"Lloyd, I'm overcome with how much God loves us. That's what I'm going to think about when I pray this part of the Lord's Prayer."

From *The Other Jesus,* by Lloyd J. Ogilvie, copyright 1986; used by permission of Word Books, Publisher, Waco, Tex.

Chapter 3

"I see by your résumé that you're highly qualified as an abstract mathematical theorist and as an expert in all aspects of the physical sciences . . . big deal, so's my calculator."

. . . **Judging Others**

by Stephen M. Miller

Background Scripture: Matthew 7:1-5; John 8:1-11

I'M AN EDITOR, dumber than most editors, because I assigned myself this chapter.

My motives were sincere. I knew this was going to be a tough assignment because it's an area in which most people struggle, myself included. But I figured this would give me a chance to research what others have said about the matter, do some serious thinking of my own, and then reflect on how I could apply all this to my life.

You see, I need the help, for I'm in the business of judging people. Though I'm not in the business of judging the spiritual condition of others, I'm one rung below that. I judge the capabilities of others and the worth of their labors. I'm a professional critic.

I decide not to give a certain West Coast writer an assignment on an article with a close deadline because this fellow couldn't meet a deadline if you promised him wealth, fame, and glory (none of which is available through writing for religious publications). And when another writer sends his stuff in, I decide whether it's acceptable or should be sent to a child day-care center so toddlers can draw stick figures on the back to justify the sacrifice of the tree.

I have several obstacles I need to overcome as I offer you my thoughts about judging others.

First, I have to explain what Jesus taught. That's not too hard. Jesus was pretty clear.

Second, I have to help you apply this to your life. That's harder. When Jesus talked about judging others, He was referring to legalistic folk who were preoccupied with the spiritual blemishes of others. We use "judging others" more broadly. For us it might not have anything to do with sin. It can simply refer to criticism—like office workers who gripe, perhaps with justification, that their supervisors are mutants who have large mouths but no ears.

To complicate this second obstacle, legalism doesn't appear to me to be as prevalent today as it was in Christ's day. It still exists; and where it does, it is as oppressive, unfair, and unchristlike as ever. But a bigger problem today seems to be the flip side of the coin: reckless freedom—believers who tend to ignore their own sins and the sins of others.

So it's a tall order to apply to free-spirited believers the message of Christ to rule-minded traditionalists.

Third, and toughest of all, is to give you some advice without turning into a hypocrite or adding several inches to my nose.

Let's look first at what Jesus taught.

What Jesus Taught About Judging Others

Jesus taught through words and actions.

To the masses on a Galilean hillside came these words during the Sermon on the Mount. "Do not judge, or you too will be judged. For in the same way you judge others, you will be judged, and with the measure you use, it will be measured to you" (Matthew 7:1-2).

Jesus wasn't calling for the elimination of all judgment on spiritual matters. If He had been, Paul would have had no right to rebuke Peter for refusing to eat with Gentiles (Galatians 2:11-14). Nor would Paul have had the right to order the Corinthian church to expel from membership the man who was living in incest with his father's wife (1 Corinthians 5:1, 13). And Paul certainly would have had no right to order the Corinthian believers not to "associate with anyone who calls himself a brother but is sexually immoral or greedy, an idolater or a slanderer, a drunkard or a swindler. With such a man do not even eat" (v. 11).

These were blatant sins, or in Peter's case certainly at least a serious error in judgment. But they were public problems that had to be dealt with publicly, and fairly.

Jesus wasn't talking about these. He was talking about vicious and unfair judgments. This becomes clear in Matthew 7:2, which says that if we tend not to give people the benefit of the doubt when we judge them, others will tend to judge us as unkindly. And if we are compassionate in our judgment of others, people will tend to be compassionate toward us. We reap what we sow. New Testament scholar Ralph Earle sums it up this way: "'You get what you give.' Give a smile and you get a smile; give a growl and you get a growl."[1]

In another scene from the Gospels, Jesus actually called for religious leaders to pass judgment. When these leaders criticized Him for healing on the Sabbath, He replied, "Stop judging by mere appearances, and make a right judgment" (John 7:24). In other words, "Think hard about this matter before you condemn Me as a sinner."

These leaders were referring to a law that went beyond the laws recorded in the Bible. The Lord, through Moses, had said we are to honor the Sabbath. But over the centuries, religious leaders added laws designed to spell out *how* to honor the Sabbath. Though the laws were oral and weren't compiled in writing until about 200 years after Christ, Jewish religious leaders of the first century knew the laws well. And these men treated the laws as sacred—just as sacred as Scripture.

The law Jesus broke was one that said you should not heal a person on the Sabbath unless the immediate situation is life-threatening. But Jesus called the group's attention to an inconsistency between this law and another Sabbath law. He referred to the Bible's allowance for breaking the Sabbath to circumcise a boy, if the eighth day of the boy's life fell on the Sabbath.

In a clever argument that abounded with insight, Jesus explained that the Bible allowed for circumcision on the Sabbath—the taking of a whole body and making it less than whole by clipping away part of it. But the oral law of the rabbis did not allow for a body to be restored to wholeness on the Sabbath. Clearly the oral law needed to be rewritten to allow for more compassion.

Jesus not only talked about judgment but passed judgment. To religious leaders who were corrupt, self-serving men who passed themselves off as godly, Jesus said, "You hypocrites! Isaiah was right when he prophesied about you: 'These people honor me with their lips, but their hearts are far from me'" (Matthew 15:7-8).

To merchants who were conducting an Oriental bazaar in the Temple courtyard, which served as the sanctuary for Gentile believers, Jesus said, "Is it not written: 'My house will be called a house of prayer for all nations'? But you have made it 'a den of robbers'" (Mark 11:17).

To men who arrested a woman caught in adultery, Jesus said, "If any one of you is without sin, let him be the first to throw a stone at her" (John 8:7).

Then He asked the woman, "Where are they? Has no one condemned you?"

"No one, sir," she said.

"Then neither do I condemn you. . . . Go now and leave your life of sin" (vv. 10-11).

So in words and action, Jesus encouraged judgment that was compassionate, well thought out, and founded on biblical principles such as respect for God's house and concern for those who seek the Lord.

Four Reasons to Be Kind in Judging Others

If your world is anything like mine, you probably don't have many people whispering to you things like, "She's not right with the Lord. She goes to the movies." Or, "He's a fake. He drinks wine with his meals."

What you're more likely to hear are judgments not related to the spiritual condition of others: criticisms about taste in clothing, instant evaluations of another's personality. And even though Jesus was probably not talking about these when He cautioned us against judging, He certainly presented us with some crossover principles we can easily apply to these.

To legalists all too eager to condemn someone as a sinner, Jesus said, "Be kind." And to believers who are sometimes just as eager to offer their expert opinion about another person or that person's work, Jesus says, "Be kind."

Why should we be kind?

1. We're not Jesus. We can't see into the hearts of other people and figure out why they are the way they are.

But we can try. And when we do, our judgments soften. Sociologist Anthony Campolo tells the story of elementary school teacher Miss Thompson. She didn't like Teddy Stallard. His clothes were musty, and his hair was unkempt. He was homely. He wore a blank expression on his face, he spoke as seldom as possible, and he didn't seem interested in school. Miss Thompson really seemed to enjoy marking *F*'s at the top of his papers.

Teddy's records didn't change her judgment of the boy, though they certainly revealed something about why he was the way he was.

First Grade: Teddy shows promise with his work and attitude, but poor home situation.

Second Grade: Teddy could do better. Mother is seriously ill. He receives little help at home.

Third Grade: Teddy is a good boy, but too serious. He is a slow learner. His mother died this year.

Fourth Grade: Teddy is very slow but well-behaved. His father shows no interest.

In spite of these notes from Teddy's previous teachers, Miss Thompson showed no special compassion for the boy. Christmas came, and the children brought presents for their teacher. On one box wrapped in brown paper were the words "For Miss Thompson from Teddy." When the teacher opened the present, out fell a gaudy rhinestone bracelet with half the stones missing, and a bottle of cheap perfume.

The kids began to giggle, but Miss Thompson put on the bracelet and dabbed some perfume on her wrist. Holding her wrist out to the children around her, she said, "Doesn't it smell lovely?" And they all agreed it did.

After school, Teddy stayed behind, then shuffled up to his teacher's desk. "Miss Thompson. Miss Thompson, you smell just like my mother. And her bracelet looks real pretty on you too. I'm glad you liked my presents."

In that moment, a teacher saw the heart of a hurting little boy. It changed not only her judgment of Teddy but also her attitude toward other children who were having trouble in school.

Another example of our inability to see beneath the surface and into the hearts and motivation of people is the case of Baptist preacher Charles Spurgeon.

He lived in England during the late 1800s. In addition to pastoring a large church that seated 6,000, Spurgeon found time to raise chickens and sell the eggs. In some circles he became known as a greedy man, not because he did a little moonlighting with chickens, but because he simply refused to give away any of the eggs. They were available for sale, but they were never free—not even to close relatives.

Spurgeon was aware of this criticism, but he didn't try to defend himself. He just went on selling eggs.

The beneath-the-surface part of the story came out only years later: All the profits from the sale of the eggs went to a couple of impoverished, elderly widows. Spurgeon had kept quiet because he didn't want to embarrass the two women.

2. Some problems we see in others may be problems we have ourselves.

We tend to see in others flaws we have. Did you ever go to a dress-up event and realize, when it was too late, you forgot to clean your shoes? And once you got to where you were going, didn't you find yourself looking at the shoes walking around you?

The same thing happens when we evaluate people. The flaws that stick out most are the ones we are most acquainted with—the flaws we have. I have an editor friend who always complains about certain writers who can't meet deadlines. But when this editor writes for publications I'm associated with, his copy is usually the latest of the lot—often two and three months overdue.

People with tempers shake their heads in disgust at exasperated parents scolding a child in the church foyer. Tightfisted people notice those who don't give to the worthy cause for which the tight fists released a couple of dollars. Opinionated people get angry when other opinionated folks don't agree with them.

When we become alert to this tendency of ours to see in others the mirrored flaws of ourselves, our judgments begin to soften.

3. First impressions can be dead wrong.

Because people can be swayed by things like appearance and dress, the ancient Greeks used to try the more complicated cases in the dark.

Henry Potter, a New York bishop in the early 1900s, told how he unfairly judged someone on the basis of appearance.

When the bishop boarded a transatlantic liner for Europe, he met the man with whom he would share a room. After spending a few minutes with the fellow, the bishop went to the purser and asked to leave his gold watch and other valuables in the ship's safe. He explained that ordinarily he never did this, but his roommate didn't look trustworthy.

The purser took the valuables, then said, "It's all right, Bishop. I'll be very glad to take care of them for you. The other man has been up here and left his for the same reason."

We live in a world that lauds instant analysis and critique. But hasty judgments of people aren't reliable, even when so-called experts are doing the judging. Consider these judgments from supposed experts, recorded for posterity in *The Experts Speak,* by Christopher Cerf and Victor Navasky (Pantheon).

To Clint Eastwood, during a 1959 meeting with a Universal Pictures executive: "You have a chip on your tooth, your Adam's apple sticks out too far, and you talk too slow." Eastwood went on to become one of the movie industry's biggest box-office attractions.

To Elvis Presley, as he was being fired by the manager of the Grand Ole Opry after one performance in 1954: "You ain't goin' nowhere . . . Son. You ought to go back to drivin' a truck."

To Rev. Jim Jones, in a 1977 letter of reference by then Vice President Walter Mondale, a letter Jones presented to the government of Guyana, where the People's Temple leader set up a religious commune: "Knowing of your congregation's deep involvement in the major social and constitutional issues of our country is a great inspiration to me." On November 18, 1978, Jones ordered his followers to drink cyanide-laced punch. Death toll was 913, including 276 children.

4. Our judgments can come back to haunt us.

French essayist and student of the classics Michel de Montaigne (mohn-TANE-yah, 1533-92) told the grim story of what happened to a Persian judge who accepted a bribe, then rendered an unjust verdict. The king, Cambysses (kam-BIE-seez, sixth century B.C.), ordered the judge executed and skinned. The judge's flesh was then tanned and used to upholster the chair on which other judges sat—a potent reminder to keep judgments fair.

Perhaps one reason we're so quick to pass unkind judgments on coworkers, relatives, acquaintances, people we hardly know, and even complete strangers is because we think we don't have to answer for our words. Chances are no one will challenge what we say, and certainly no one is going to tan our hide and tack it to the love seat.

But harsh judgments that serve no redeeming purpose are remembered: by the ones who heard them and who may one day pronounce judgment on us, and by the One who shares the pain of His creation who has endured the unjust tongue-lashing.

A Final Word

Nearly every day I'm called on—or tempted—to express a personal opinion about someone. For I work elbow to elbow with ministers who don't minister, teachers who don't teach, and assistants who don't assist.

Even so, the single truth I'm trying to learn to live by when it comes to passing judgment on others is that I don't have all the facts. Poet Henry Wadsworth Longfellow once said that if we could read the secret history of our enemies, we would find in each person's life enough sorrow and suffering to disarm all hostility.

I have a theory about how Christians are going to be able to get along in heaven when they can't get along down here. My theory is that when we reach heaven, we'll all know one another the way Jesus knows us. And as a result, we'll love one another the way Jesus loves us. For as William and Gloria Gaither's song puts it so well, "The One who knows us best loves us most."[2] That's a good thing to remember when we're tempted to judge someone.

There will come times when we have to pass judgment on others. Employees need to be evaluated, defendants need to be tried, and occasionally church members need to be disciplined. But in our judgment, perhaps it would be good to remember the words of a poet whose name has been lost in decades past.

> Pray don't find fault with a man who limps
>   Or stumbles along the road,
> Unless you have worn the shoes he wears
>   Or struggled beneath his load.
>
> There may be tacks in his shoes that hurt,
>   Though hidden away from view;
> Or the burden he bears, placed on your back,
>   Might cause you to stumble, too.

Don't sneer at the man who is down today,
　Unless you have felt the blow
That caused his fall, or felt the shame
　That only the fallen know.

You may be strong, but still the blows
　That were his, if dealt to you
In the selfsame way at the selfsame time,
　Might cause you to stagger, too.

Don't be too harsh with a man who sins,
　Or pelt him with words or stones,
Unless you are sure, yea, doubly sure,
　That you have not sins of your own.

For you know, perhaps, if the tempter's voice
　Should whisper as soft to you
As it did to him when he went astray,
　'Twould cause you to falter, too.

---

1. Ralph Earle, "Matthew," *Beacon Bible Commentary* (Kansas City: Beacon Hill Press of Kansas City, 1964), 6:87.

2. From "I Am Loved," by William J. and Gloria Gaither, ©copyright 1978 by William J. Gaither. All rights reserved. Used by permission.

Stephen M. Miller edits the Dialog Series of books.

Chapter 4

Dear Grandma,
Thank you for the tape recorder you sent for Christmas. I have already made quite a bit of money selling tapes I've made around the house on Sunday mornings. I am saving up to buy a video camera.
Thank you again.
Love,
Eldon

. . . the Sabbath

by Ed Robinson

Background Scripture: Exodus 20:8-11; Deuteronomy 5:12-15; Mark 2:23—3:6

CHRISTIANS TODAY have strange ways of honoring the Sabbath and keeping it holy.

• Some beat the sun in rising, spend most of the day at Sunday School, morning worship, choir practice, evening worship, and an afterglow. Then, in the darkness, they return home as burnt-out bodies that collapse into bed.

• Some attend morning worship, then spend the rest of the day relaxing in front of a TV tube, watching full-grown men in helmets run into each other.

• Others attend the morning services, return home to lunch and a sanctified nap, go to the evening services, then return home for popcorn and the Sunday night movie on TV.

It's pretty clear that Christians don't agree on how to honor the Sabbath. But that's not a new problem.

A Little History

People called Sabbatarians (sab-ah-TER-ee-ans, known for their elaborate Sabbath rules) have appeared in every period of church history from the time of Christ to the modern era. For example, they show up in the writings of the church before and during the medieval period. According to the rules spelled out at the Synod of Elvira in Spain (A.D. 306), if you missed three consecutive Sundays from church, you could be excommunicated. (Think what an impact that might have on church attendance today.)

By the 16th century an elaborate system of rules for church attendance had emerged to the point where it was determined how late you could come to church and still be counted as present. A modern equivalent would allow a person to come halfway through the sermon and still be counted in the morning attendance figures.

In the mid-1600s, the Puritans of England developed a rule book governing the Sabbath activities. Rules covered issues such as how far a person could travel on the Sabbath, how to dress, and which homemaking activities were acceptable. By 1656 these rules took up about 13 pages of fine print.

Some of these same Sabbath rules later found their way to the New World and became part of the practice of the church, especially in New England. And many of those rules have lived on—at least in spirit—through the last three centuries in both civil and religious codes. The "blue laws" in some areas are a civil expression of these Sabbath rules. Alongside these civil codes are the written and unwritten practices of Christians.

Many sincere Christians, for example, will not read a newspaper or watch television on Sunday. Others will not buy any unnecessary products on Sunday, including food at a restaurant. Following the Puritan practice of resting on the Sabbath, many Christians take a Sunday afternoon nap. Some Christians believe that Sunday should be given entirely to spiritual activities. So they spend the entire day in worship, study, prayer, and meditation.

So the question of how to honor the Sabbath is incredibly important to many Christians. On the flip side of the coin, however, Sabbath behavior is hardly an issue at all for other believers.

But somewhere between these two positions are Christians who grapple with this issue, which has been made more complex by a society that increasingly treats Sunday like any other day. Perhaps Christians like these can find a bit of direction in the way Christ viewed the host of Sabbath rules in His day.

Sabbath Rules in Christ's Day

The fourth commandment of the Ten Commandments reads,

"Remember the Sabbath day by keeping it holy. Six days you shall labor and do all your work, but the seventh day is a Sabbath to the Lord your God. On it you shall not do any work, neither you, nor your son or daughter, not your manservant or maidservant, nor your animals, nor the alien within your gates. For in six days the Lord made the heavens and the earth, the sea, and all that is in them, but he rested on the seventh day. Therefore the Lord blessed the Sabbath day and made it holy" *(Exodus 20:8-11).*

The same commandment appears in a listing of the Ten Commandments in Deuteronomy with a slight change: The commandment is tied to the deliverance of the Israelites from Egypt rather than to creation.

"Remember that you were slaves in Egypt and that the Lord your God brought you out of there with a mighty hand and an outstretched arm. Therefore the Lord your God has commanded you to observe the Sabbath day" *(Deuteronomy 5:15).*

The Sabbath was God's gift to humanity, allowing us to (1) cease from regular labors as God ceased from the labor of creation, and (2) to celebrate His deliverance of the Israelites from slavery. Sabbath was a gift of grace, not an imposition of law.

The observance of the Sabbath became one of the trademarks of Judaism. It was observed from sundown on Friday to sundown on Saturday. But during their 70 years of exile in Babylon, in the late sixth century B.C., many Jews lost touch with the Hebrew language and literature. So when they returned to Israel and the Scriptures were read in the public assemblies, many needed an interpreter (see Nehemiah 8:8).

It was this need for the interpreter that propelled the scribe into prominence in Hebrew society. The scribe became the main authority on the law of Moses. Consequently, as questions concerning the Sabbath law emerged, so did a complex system of rules to govern almost every situation.

For example, these religious leaders established the following Sabbath rules.

• People were not permitted to pick a single stalk of grain and rub it in their hands to retrieve the kernels, as Jesus did. Technically, this was considered harvesting.

• The distance a person was permitted to travel on the Sabbath was 2,000 paces, about three-quarters of a mile. To travel farther was a sin.

• Because Jeremiah had preached against carrying "burdens" on the Sabbath, the scribes decided to establish exactly what a burden was. They determined it was equivalent to the weight of a dried fig. Since nails were heavier than dried figs, it was considered sinful on the Sabbath to wear shoes that had been manufactured with nails.

• Walking in the grass was on the list of evil acts, because this was considered threshing.

• Dipping a radish in salt and letting it remain for anything longer than a quick dip was forbidden, since this constituted pickling—which, of course, was work.

It was into such a world of endlessly intricate rules that Jesus expressed His views about the Sabbath.

Jesus and the Sabbath

Jesus preached no long sermons concerning the Sabbath. And He told no parable to unlock the mysteries of what people should or should not do on the Sabbath. But He certainly expressed His views about the Sabbath through His actions.

1. Jesus gave priority to the celebration of salvation and worship on the Sabbath. Sabbath was a day of worship for the Jews. During certain times of the year devout Jews would go to worship every day, but the Sabbath was a consistent day of worship throughout the year. Jesus, too, made it a practice to worship on the Sabbath. When Jesus returned to His hometown of Nazareth, He went to the synagogue on the Sabbath "as was his custom" (Luke 4:16).

The Early Church continued this priority of worship. With the Sunday resurrection of Jesus, the Church began to gather on that day of the week to worship and celebrate. The Jewish Christians, however, observed both the Jewish Sabbath and the Christian "Lord's Day." Though the Gentile believers didn't follow the Jewish Sabbath observance, they did make their Sunday their "Sabbath," or day of worship and celebration. With the decree of Roman emperor Constantine in A.D. 321, Sunday received official sanction. Yet the decree simply formalized what had become an established practice of Christian worship.

2. Jesus did good works on the Sabbath. "It is lawful to do good on the Sabbath" (Matthew 12:12). The Bible records several accounts of Jesus healing and casting out demons on the Sabbath. And in almost every account Jesus responded to human need in the face of opposition from the Pharisees. In each instance Jesus emphasized that healing was in keeping with the spirit of the Sabbath.

In response to the Pharisees' criticism concerning healing a crippled woman, Jesus said, "You hypocrites! Doesn't each of you on the Sabbath untie his ox or donkey from the stall and lead it out to give it water? Then should not this woman, a daughter of Abraham, whom Satan has kept bound for eighteen long years, be set free on the Sabbath day from what bound her?" (Luke 13:15-16).

We have traditionally seen Sunday as a day of rest and worship. Perhaps it is time for us to rediscover the Sabbath practice of "doing good" in response to human need: visiting the lonely, helping the poor, feeding the hungry, or caring for the sick.

3. Jesus viewed the Sabbath as a gift of God, not legalistic bondage. The Gospel writers recorded the Sabbath activities of Jesus on purpose. One of the most notable of these stories was that of Jesus and the disciples picking a few stalks of grain and eating the kernels. When the legalists of Jesus' day saw this "desecration" of the Sabbath, they responded with accusations.

Jesus answered the Pharisees by pronouncing that the Sabbath was not introduced as a slavelike bondage for the people, but that the Sabbath was created as a gift from God to benefit humanity. To chain people to a Sabbath day that allowed no healing, celebration, or ministry to others would be a cruel trick. God didn't design such a trick. "The Sabbath was made for man, not man for the Sabbath. So the Son of Man is Lord even of the Sabbath" (Mark 2:27-28).

At times, the easiest way to make decisions is to have someone else make them for you. In this modern era, many have asked their church leaders to make decisions for them concerning what is appropriate activity for Sunday. In response, and in order to cover all the possible situations, some denominations and local churches have generated rules about how to honor the Lord's day. Unfortunately, this new legalism is not too unlike the legalism of Jesus' day, that system of rules against which He spoke so passionately.

I believe we do well to select Sunday activities according to the principles of Scripture and the life of Jesus, rather than according to an artificially constructed rule book.

I realize that these three principles from the life of Jesus do not offer concrete answers to many of the questions Christians ask about their activities on Sunday. It probably would have been easier for many to have someone say, "No working on Sunday," "No eating out on Sunday," "No going to the grocery store on Sunday (except in emergencies)," "No reading the paper or watching TV on Sunday," "No playing sports on Sunday," and on and on and on. But to create such a list is to create another legalism.

Each Christian has to come to grips with the message of Jesus concerning the Sabbath. This is not to say that a Christian should treat Sunday as any other day of the week. No, priority must be given on the Lord's day to worship, celebration, and ministry. If we are to follow the example of Jesus, we will find ourselves involved in these tasks. Perhaps if we engage in these primary activities of the Sabbath, we won't have either the desire or the time for the less important activities or for worrying about what we should or should not be doing.

Ed Robinson is an assistant professor of religious education at Nazarene Theological Seminary, Kansas City.

Chapter 5

... the Poor

by Bryan Stone

Background Scripture: Matthew 25:31-46; Luke 4:18-19; 18:18-25

MY WIFE, CHERYL, and I minister in a Fort Worth inner-city church called Liberation Community. Just a few weeks after we moved into the neighborhood, we realized we had a big choice to make. We could become part of the inner city and the lives of the people who live here, or we could remain comfortable and insulated by a standard of living that was quite different from that of our neighbors.

Cheryl was especially aware of this because she had just been given a $200 outfit. She could choose to wear it and protect it from the dirty hands and greasy hair that wanted to snuggle up against it. Or she could wear something more practical and washable, and be able to enjoy the hugs and even give a few.

Cheryl could also choose to spend money and time to make the inside of our house look like the cover of *Better Homes and Gardens,* and keep the children of the neighborhood confined to our backyard or the utility room. Or she could spend money and time reading books with the children, making birthday cakes with them in the kitchen, and helping them with their homework in our living room.

Cheryl is a living example of how an intense desire to participate in the lives of the poor has resulted in a change of life-style, a change of priorities, and a change of values. If we are really serious about doing more than simply giving away "charity" to the poor, we must involve ourselves in the lives of those who suffer from economic deprivation—and that means removing the barriers between us and them. Nothing creates or sustains those barriers more than a life-style that distances one group from another.

The first word in ministry to the poor must be *life-style.*

Jesus Pledged His Allegiance to the Poor

Both the words and actions of Jesus bear this out. Not only was Jesus poor but also He voluntarily took on the life-style of poverty. Though He was born in a manger, it was into the family of a carpenter, not exactly the lowliest of occupations in the world at that time (or in ours).

Even so, from the very beginning of His ministry He clearly spelled out where His allegiances lay. His first sermon was in His home city of Nazareth. Nearly all His relatives, childhood friends, and the respected leaders of the community who had watched Him grow up were probably in the synagogue that Sabbath morning. Jesus stood up to speak and chose a passage from the prophet Isaiah:

"The Spirit of the Lord is upon Me, because He anointed Me to preach the gospel to the poor. He has sent Me to proclaim release to the captives, and recovery of sight to the blind, to set free those who are downtrodden, to proclaim the favorable year of the Lord" *(Luke 4:18-19, NASB).*

Jesus was casting His lot with the poor. He was taking sides. In fact, Jesus went on in His sermon to cite the example of Elijah the prophet who came not to the rich and powerful but to a poor widow woman.

Jesus was siding with the poor, just as His Father had done in Old Testament times. Throughout the Bible, whenever there was oppression, exploitation, injustice; wherever there were people accumulating wealth while those around them suffered and became ground up under the wheel of poverty, God was found taking sides with the oppressed and against the oppressor. God was *for* the children of Israel and *against* Pharaoh and Pharaoh's mighty armies.

Today's church is much like the group that congregated in Nazareth to hear Jesus' first sermon. We want to help the poor, and we are struggling to find ways to do just that. Too often, however, when helping the poor means taking sides, or identifying ourselves with a different crowd, we step back. When the message of Jesus goes beyond "preaching the gospel to the poor" and becomes "identifying with the poor," or "participating in the suffering of the poor," we turn down the volume or simply switch channels.

What Jesus was pointing to, I think, is that our relationship to the poor should be something more than just pity or charity. It is a matter of adjusting our life-styles. True compassion for the poor means giving more than just our dollars. It means giving ourselves.

Of course, it is easier to send a check or to hold a fundraiser (important as this is) than to find ways of identifying with those who suffer because of poverty. But so far as Christianity goes, there is no substitute.

One women's ministries group I know of has found a way to move beyond charity and toward true compassion. Barbara and several of her friends made up the women's ministries fellowship in a nearby suburban church in our city. They had been supportive in donating clothing and often money to the ministries of Liberation Community. One day, however, they decided to come down and work for a day.

What a transformation! To experience the needs firsthand, to hear the stories, and to see the faces of those in desperate economic circumstances made an impact that would be difficult to erase. Soon the women were spending more and more time in the inner city. Instead of spending their spare time and money on themselves, they began to sponsor needy families in the inner city.

They did more than just send a check. They got to know an elderly woman named Charlene along with her three children. Charlene and her family live one day to the next, trying to make ends meet. However, Barbara and her friends got into Charlene's life and got to know her situation. When Christmas came around, joy and smiles filled Charlene's house as Barbara and company brought Christmas presents, a Christmas tree, and a hot Christmas dinner to Charlene's house.

This relationship continued beyond Christmas. The women constantly check on the family and share their warmth and love. There is no substitute for firsthand knowledge of someone's needs. This firsthand knowledge of the needs of the poor, of course, means being where they are. And, as in the case of Barbara and her friends, that meant a change in their own life-styles.

Jesus Clearly Identified the Poor

In Jesus' short statement of His mission, He identified the several groups to whom He feels especially called; and each group involves the poor. Jesus, of course, specifically mentioned "the poor." And here He was referring to the economically deprived group that made up most of Palestine's population in the first century.

Jesus also mentioned "the captives." The poor can sometimes withstand the pressure of poverty for a little while if they can only envision some way of escape, if they can muster hope for a brighter day. When Jesus talked about captives, He was referring to those who felt trapped, with little or no prospects for escape from their misery and oppression.

Some of these were literally prisoners in cells. But most of them would not have been imprisoned because of crimes, but because of debts. When Jesus turned His attention to the poor and the captives, he was referring not to two separate groups but to one: the poor. For captivity was too often the result of poverty.

One woman, Anita, came to our ministry very much a captive. She had been living in Waco with her 11 children and an abusive husband. One night, after he beat her with a gun, she and her children fled. She drove to Fort Worth, where her brother arranged for her to stay for a few days in an unrented house.

When Anita and her children arrived in town, they had no money and only the clothes on their backs. So in the unfurnished house they all slept on the floor, while the baby slept in a cardboard box. The future looked dim, and the bars of Anita's prison looked solid.

But as she was driving through our neighborhood one day, she saw our sign: Liberation Community. And she decided to come in, for she had nothing to lose. Through the help of some generous Christians, we were able to give Anita food, clothing, and furniture. The owner of the house agreed to rent it to her. And through the connections of one of our church members, we were able to get the gas turned on for heating. A short time later, Anita found a job.

Not only did Anita hear the Good News but also she experienced it. She had found a community of people who helped her feel good about herself, and she found a place of healing for some very deep wounds. The gospel brings liberation to the prisoner.

Jesus also describes the poor as "oppressed." It is important for us to realize, as Jesus did, that so many of the poor are poor, not because of their laziness, because of misfortune, or because of underdevelopment. They are poor because of oppression.

The poor, as a group, are so often those who have been locked out, robbed of opportunity, and trampled upon by those in power. Perhaps the reason is skin color, nationality, education, age, or gender. But one of the root causes of poverty is oppression and injustice.

Many injustices are difficult to point to specifically. But let me try. Very few middle-income or high-income families will feel the financial pinch of paying for driver's training for their children, which costs over $200 in our city. Low-income families, however, simply cannot afford this fee. So hundreds of inner-city young people never take driver's education.

It doesn't take us long to figure out the consequences of this kind of "invisible" injustice; it reinforces the cycle of poverty and helplessness. The lack of a driver's license decreases a person's ability to be mobile. And whether we like it or not, in our society we need dependable transportation in order to find a job and keep it.

Injustice like this makes it impossible for the poor, on their own, to rise above the odds against them. Unless we are sensitive to the cries of those who live life in a social system that is stacked against them, the gospel will become only a gospel of the wealthy and the powerful.

Jesus goes on to single out "the blind" as part of the same group we could call the poor. What we have to remember is that in the time of Jesus, begging and blindness went hand in hand. In fact, six of the seven blind people Luke mentions were poor.

So Jesus broadens our concept of evangelism by making it include good news for the poor, liberation for the captive, vision for the blind—and, finally, a revolution in the way we order our society.

This revolution is revealed in the final phrase Jesus used to describe His ministry. He used the prophet's words "to proclaim the favorable year of the Lord" (NASB), a clear reference to the jubilee year in which all debts were to be canceled, all slaves freed, and all land returned to its original owners. This was to be nothing short of a social revolution in the land every 7 years and, on a grander scale, every 50 years.

The point is: Our involvement with the poor is to go beyond mere charity and is to include justice in how we order our society.

As Christians, we have a responsibility to see to it that the poor and defenseless are empowered and given opportunity in our society. This empowerment may come in many areas, including employment and education. At Liberation Community, I have witnessed an example of this kind of empowerment through a program called Project Power.

Vickie came to the church, seeking emergency food assistance. She was a single parent of two young children. She was unemployed and had recently been subpoenaed for writing a series of bad checks. Vickie needed more than a sack of groceries. Forrest Whitlow, our director of Project Power, first helped Vickie get free legal advice, to keep her out of jail. She did not have the money to cover the bad checks right away, but through the help of the lawyer she was able to work out a payment plan and avoid jail.

Next, Vickie entered our Job Club; and after a couple of weeks of hard work and a lot of encouragement, she found a job at Sears. Soon her oldest daughter enrolled in Liberation Club, our Saturday School for children. Then Vickie began attending our church and now is volunteering time during the week to help in our emergency assistance food distribution each Friday.

Vickie is evidence that the good news from God extends to every facet of life and is able to transform and empower people. This good news turns people from lives of dependency and disappointment to lives of responsibility and joy.

Jesus Says Our Salvation Depends on Our Helping the Poor

It is so important to see in Jesus' words how important He felt ministry to the poor was. It was not just some interesting sidelight in Jesus' ministry. In fact, at one point when John the Baptist sent his disciples to Jesus to ask if He was the Messiah, Jesus referred to ministry to the poor as one of the signs of His Messiahship (Matthew 11:5).

Perhaps the most interesting, revealing, and shocking of Jesus' statements regarding the poor are those in which He connects the poor to salvation. In some instances, Jesus revealed, it is the poor who model the path of salvation. For example, Jesus refers to the poor as "blessed" and says that theirs is "the kingdom of God" (Luke 6:20). In other instances, it is our own involvement with the poor that determines the path for our own salvation.

Very few times do we have record in the Bible of anyone actually asking Jesus point blank: "How can I get saved?" But the example of the rich young ruler is one such incident. So far as the Law was concerned, the man had done well. He had kept the commandments from his childhood. But that wasn't enough. Jesus gave him the final requirement: Go and sell all you have and give the money to the poor.

In other words, personal piety didn't cut it when it came to his salvation. It was not enough, for he had placed his money before God. We must also have a concern for those in need and a commitment to using our resources to meet those needs. This is a central and, indeed, essential dimension to what it means to be a Christian. In a very real sense, it is a vital aspect of what salvation involves.

It is not surprising that Jesus' words to the rich young ruler are so often bracketed and placed under the category of "exception sayings"—that is, those sayings of Jesus that do not apply to most of us and that hold true only in special circumstances.

But creative treatment of Jesus' words, though not surprising, is hardly justified. Not only does it arbitrarily exempt most of us from Christ's hard words, but also it clearly runs contrary to another passage of Scripture in which Jesus, again, is dealing with our salvation.

In Matthew 25, Jesus revealed the criteria by which God will distinguish between the saved and the damned at the Judgment Seat.

Jesus presents an image of the King sitting on His throne, with the nations gathered before Him. The King separates the sheep (or the saved) to the right and the goats (or the damned) to the left. And He does it with the following words:

"Come, you who are blessed of My Father, inherit the kingdom prepared for you from the foundation of the world. For I was hungry, and you gave Me something to eat; I was thirsty, and you gave Me drink; I was a stranger, and you invited Me in; naked, and you clothed Me; I was sick, and you visited Me; I was in prison, and you came to Me" *(Matthew 25:34-36, NASB).*

Here again, Jesus demonstrated that the gospel is thoroughly social and that entrance into the Kingdom is not to stop with a private affair between the individual and God. Salvation involves our neighbor, and it specifically includes attending to the basic needs of the people around us who are hurting.

When Jesus talked about the poor, then, He was not talking about some "other" group "over there" on the other side of town. He was announcing with whom He had cast

His lot. He was declaring where God would be found and to whom we must pay special attention in working out our own salvation.

Who the poor are may be difficult to determine sometimes. We all have needs. Nevertheless, it is clear that Christ made His home among, and directed His ministry to, those who struggled with the basic necessities of life: food, clothing, and shelter.

As followers of Christ we cannot reduce "accepting" Christ to a private, spiritual decision of the heart. To "accept" Christ means accepting, as our own, His way of life and His mission.

Bryan Stone is pastor of Liberation Community Church of the Nazarene, Fort Worth.

Chapter 6

"No, ma'am, I'm not a preacher.
I've just been ill for a few days."

. . . **Healing**

by David F. Nixon

*Background Scripture: John 9:1-12; James 5:13-16;
2 Corinthians 12:7-10*

WHILE I WAS on a pastoral visit, someone asked me,
"Have you ever known anyone who, really, was healed?"

I have anointed with oil and prayed for the healing of
people with various physical needs. Many of those people

later testified to God's healing touch. But many others who were anointed and prayed for were not healed.

The late Dr. Don Gibson, once executive secretary of the Evangelism Department for the Church of the Nazarene, began every correspondence with the affirmation, "Isn't God good?" But the good God he served did not see fit to reverse the cancer that later took Dr. Gibson's life. Likewise, Rev. Gerald Green, a successful pastor and leader in my denomination, died of leukemia in 1982. The year before, the General Board had special prayer for him. General Superintendent Jerald Johnson was anointed on behalf of Rev. Green. And the pastor improved dramatically. His leukemia went into remission. But a year later he died.

But on the other side of the issue of healing, the Overland Church of the Nazarene in St. Louis still talks about the revival with evangelist Nettie Miller. During that service a woman whose leg was severely burned by contact with a hot motorcycle muffler saw her leg healed instantly. In that same revival a girl's teeth were straightened in answer to prayer.

Why are some healed when we pray, and not others?

Our Preoccupation with Physical Health

Our world is preoccupied with physical health. More attention is given to health and fitness than ever before. Rightly or wrongly, we have come to believe that good health is the inalienable right of all good citizens.

We are continually dazzled by the marvels of modern medicine. Our doctors and scientists are committed to the total abolishment of ill health. Progress has been phenomenal.

Why do we exercise and do all the other things that make for better bodily health? Are we chasing a dream of never having to be sick? Do we believe that a pain-free, disability-free life is our right?

Sickness leading toward death is a fact of life humans

have encountered ever since the Fall. Had there been no sin, there would have been no sickness. But sin is universal, and sickness is one of the results.

That any recovery is made from any illness or injury is miraculous. One writer observes that:

> In the ordinary course of things we should be eaten alive by bacteria, consumed by cancer, clogged up by fats and clots, eroded by acids. It is hardly remarkable that we sicken and die; what is truly remarkable is that we don't usually sicken very often and we don't die very quickly.[1]

We are quick to question the goodness of God when we experience ill health. But that we live as long as we do is testimony to God's sustaining grace in our lives. Does this mean we should resign ourselves to sickness and disease, and consider ourselves blessed to be alive? Or do believers have a right to ask God for healing?

Jesus' Interest in Physical Healing

New Testament writers record no less than 45 instances of healing by Jesus during His life and ministry. Twenty-six of these were healing miracles performed upon individuals. Nineteen other healing miracles involved groups of people.

The kinds of physical and emotional problems confronted by Jesus run the gamut of every malady from fever, malaria, leprosy, deafness, and congenital blindness, to anxiety, fear, and nervousness.

In Luke 8, a woman believed that if she could just touch the hem of His garment, she would be healed of her hemorrhage. So she did just that in the midst of a crowd. Conscious that His healing power had been released, Jesus asked, "Who touched me?" (v. 45). She touched Jesus and was healed.

Were there others who needed healing in that thronging mass of people? Probably. At the Pool of Bethesda Jesus encountered a great number of disabled people—the blind, the lame, the paralyzed. To our knowledge, only the man who had lain there 38 years received healing that day.

The healing miracles of Christ, in these two cases, fit the spiritual and redemptive purposes of God.

Jesus wasn't the only one doing healing miracles in His day. He admonished His disciples to "heal the sick . . . and tell them, 'The kingdom of God is near you'" (Luke 10:9). And in Matthew 10:1 we read, "And when he had called unto him his twelve disciples, he gave them power against unclean spirits, to cast them out, and to heal all manner of sickness and all manner of disease" (KJV).

The apostles continued the healing ministry of Jesus. Seventeen instances of healing are recorded in Acts. It was a vital part of ministry of the Church.

When believers were ill, James told them to "call the elders of the church to pray over [them] and anoint [them] with oil in the name of the Lord" (5:14). The healing ministry of the Early Church was patterned after that of Jesus.

Today, many of our churches still follow this pattern when they pray for the sick.

Although not everyone who is sick is healed, believers have a biblical right to ask for healing. The practice of anointing and praying for physical healing is an obedient response to our scriptural option.

Unbiblical Responses to Sickness

1. "What you need is more faith."

It is cruel and destructive for us to tell others that healing has been denied because of some defect in their faith. This heresy says, "Sickness is never the will of God. The devil is at work in your sickness, and God is waiting for you to muster enough faith to be healed."

Presbyterian minister Lloyd Ogilvie calls this "the more faith heresy." It is a misconception of faith to think we can generate enough faith to persuade God to heal us.

Sometimes healing is simply not in the will of God.

Sometimes God needs to communicate through hurting people to a hurting world.

2. "There must be unconfessed sin in your life."

This response is as old as the advice of Job's "friends." Their cruel reproach pushed him further into despair. On and on it goes. "You must be displeasing God." "You must have sidestepped His will in some way, or this would not be happening to you." This "blame the victim" response must also be avoided.

In John 9:1-12 the disciples asked Jesus about a man blind since birth, "Who sinned, this man or his parents, that he was born blind?" (v. 2). Jesus made it very clear that the man's condition had nothing to do with sin. Rather, his handicap would display the work of God in his life.

Christians populate hospital wards, asylums, and cancer hospices in approximate proportion to the world at large. Medical doctor Paul Brand, writing in *Christianity Today,* said,

> Many Christians who roll in wheelchairs, or awake each day to the scarred stumps of amputated limbs, or undergo the debility of spreading cancer have prayed for healing. Some have attended healing services, felt a sudden rush of hope, and kneeled for an anointing of oil; yet still they live unhealed. For them, divine healing is the cruelest joke of all. At the precise moment when they most need support from the church they receive instead a taunting accusation that in spiritual as well as physical health they do not measure up.[2]

Jesus assures us, as God assured Job, that despite persistent illness we may measure up spiritually in our relationship to Him.

3. "Your problem is that you don't praise God for your suffering."

This unrealistic response usually comes from some self-appointed spiritual cheerleader.

Ray Stedman in his *Discovery Papers* says,

Many Christians falsely believe that the Bible calls them to a grin-and-bear-it attitude that even a non-Christian can adopt when there is nothing much he can do about a situation. To listen to some of today's sermons and to read some popular books one would think that Christians are being exhorted to screw on a smile and go around saying, "Hallelujah, hallelujah, I've got cancer!"[3]

Such responses are not only unrealistic, they are unbiblical. Miraculous healing is not God's sole method of healing. Our pain is not necessarily the result of unconfessed sin, nor is it always a sign of God's displeasure with us. It is rarely a figment of our imagination. Nor can we fake jolly cheer about it. But we can cling to the simple truth that Jesus is "a man of sorrows, and familiar with suffering" (Isaiah 53:3). He will not abandon us in our hour of deepest need. "And surely I am with you always" (Matthew 28:20).

Principles We Can Live With

1. Divine Intervention

That God intervenes with divine healing cannot be denied. We have a right to ask for it. We do not have to coax God to heal us. Simply ask. As Jesus miraculously intervened in the lives of many with physical needs, God directly intervenes in ways that defy medical explanation.

The purpose for which Jesus intervened should not be overlooked. He intervened to declare that He had come to make people whole. He referred to the healings as "works," not miracles. He brought wholeness to every life He touched almost as a common, ordinary experience.

2. Partnership

A satisfying theology of healing recognizes that "all healing is of God." God often works in partnership with medical practice. Therefore, no legitimate means of healing should be discarded. Medication, surgery, physical therapy, and other medical remedies should be used in cooperation with prayer.

3. The Ultimate Healing

Honesty demands we admit that divine intervention and partnership do not always bring the desired healing. In three seasons of intensive prayer Paul prayed that his "thorn in the flesh" would be removed. Instead, God said, "My grace is sufficient for you" (2 Corinthians 12:9). God chose to use His power to sustain the apostle, rather than to take his malady away.

The ultimate healing was promised by Jesus himself when He declared, "I am the resurrection and the life. He who believes in me will live, even though he dies; and whoever lives and believes in me will never die" (John 11:25-26).

In one sense, God always heals. But we must be open to the "form" that healing may take: sudden divine intervention, gradual healing through a long process of medical treatment, or grace sufficient to endure an illness that ends in physical death. Bodily resurrection is the ultimate form of healing guaranteed by Jesus.

Steps to Healing

There are no surefire steps to healing. But since it is our privilege to ask for divine intervention, the following steps may be helpful when it comes time to ask.

1. Review the promises of God.

Search the Scriptures for verses that speak to your condition. Keep in mind that Jesus wants to heal people (see Matthew 8:2-4). He is just as able to heal as He is to forgive (9:2-8). Acknowledge Jesus' authority over all things, including sickness.

2. Repent of any unconfessed sin.

Unconfessed sin blocks the effectiveness of prayer (Psalm 66:18). Clear any obstacle preventing effective prayer by confessing and receiving the forgiveness Christ offers.

3. Request God's best for you.

Present your petition to God. Ask for anointing. Enlist prayer support from your family and friends. You are not alone in your illness. You have brothers and sisters in Christ to love you, encourage you, and stand by you with their prayers. If God's best is different from what you asked for, claim His all-sufficient grace.

A man I know of was told by his doctor that he had cancer. He went home from the hospital "to cry and to die." But as he prayed, he began to feel that he should, instead, play. So he decided to have "a cancer party."

He invited his close friends. When his guests had arrived, he called them to attention, saying, "I've been told I have terminal cancer. Then my wife and I realized, we're all terminal! We've decided to start a new organization. It's called MTC (Make Today Count). You're all charter members."

Since that time the organization has grown across America. In its founder's words he has been "too busy to die." When God does not heal, we can make today count by singing, loving, and not losing one minute of joy.

"Now we know that if the earthly tent we live in is destroyed, we have a building from God, an eternal house in heaven, not built by human hands" (2 Corinthians 5:1).

---

1. M. Scott Peck, *The Road Less Traveled* (New York: Simon and Schuster, 1978), quoted in Ron Lee Davis, *The Healing Choice* (Waco, Tex.: Word Books, 1986), 41.

2. Ibid., 39.

3. Quoted in Ron Lee Davis, *Gold in the Making* (Nashville: Thomas Nelson Publishers, 1983), 93.

David F. Nixon is pastor of Lake Avenue Church of the Nazarene, Fort Wayne, Ind.

Chapter 7

. . . Death

by Lloyd John Ogilvie

Background Scripture: Luke 16:19-31

THE FUNERAL SERVICE of a good friend lingers in my mind. My grief was not only because I had lost a friend, but because he consistently resisted becoming a Christian. Nothing that I or countless others said or did was able to break the shell of his self-sufficiency. Success and wealth insulated him from the recognition of his need. My friend acted as if he would live forever. I believe he did. My concern was where, with whom, and how.

As I sat in the funeral parlor, I looked around at the faces of his family, friends, and business associates. What did they believe about death and an afterlife? Did any of them wonder about his own death?

The service was benign. A combination of soothing music, poetry, and a eulogy that recounted my friend's accomplishments, attainments, and contributions to benevolent causes. Nothing was said about life after death. What could be said?

I wondered what my friend would have said to the gathering of loved ones and acquaintances if he had been able to return and speak about life after death. Would he have warned them, alarmed them, about what it's like to walk through the valley of the shadow of death without a Savior, and to spend eternity in the irrevocable separation from God? Accounts of those who have died and come back to life after a few moments have had great fascination for people. We wonder if any of the people whom we have known have ever wanted to come back across the great divide to tell us what they experienced after death. What would they say? Would we listen?

The rich man of Jesus' parable wanted to send a message back to his five brothers. Tradition has named him Dives (DI-vees), the Latin name for rich man. He had died and found himself in the fires of Hades. How he got there is the impelling story called the parable of Dives and Lazarus. It is a gripping drama in three acts.

Act I

Act One is a study in contrasts, a tableau of the extremities of the rich and the poor. In one sweeping sentence, Jesus characterizes Dives vividly by describing his purple and fine linen. His linen undergarment coat with long sleeves was probably made of Egyptian flax, often as valuable as gold. The cloak worn over his coat was made of costly purple material. Purple was the sign of royalty or immense wealth. The dye was obtained from the purple fish, a species of mussel, at prohibitive cost to any but the most affluent and powerful.

The way Dives lived was consistent with his clothing. "Gaily living in splendor" (Luke 16:19, NASB) are Jesus' words.

Lazarus is a startling contrast. He was "covered with sores" of leprosy. The pitiful creature seems to contradict his name, which means "God is my help." This parable is the only one in which a character is given a name. The reason will become evident as the drama unfolds. Each day Lazarus is laid at Dives' gate to beg for crumbs from the wealthy man's table. The word for gate, *pylōn* in Greek, intensifies the contrast between Dives' splendor and Lazarus' squalor. It means a gate full of magnificent artistry and exquisite beauty. From that we get a picture of what Dives' mansion must have been like. A startling backdrop for Lazarus' pitiful plight. The leper does not even have enough strength to fight off the dogs that lick his pus-oozing sores. We flinch at the vividness of Jesus' portrait.

Act One has put us on the edge of our seats. We feel the alarming distortion of life. Is there no justice? How can God allow this blasphemous inequality? The act comes to an excruciating close with our questions unanswered.

Both Lazarus and Dives die. The disposition of their bodies dramatizes the dreadful disparity of life. Lazarus' body is flung naked on the burning rubbish heap outside the city wall. Dives is buried in a tomb aboveground reserved for the wealthy and powerful. But both men are dead, nonetheless. Death, the grim reaper, is no respecter of persons or position. We feel a heaviness, an indignant anger, as the curtain drops on Act One.

Act 2

We are astonished by the revolutionary reverses portrayed as Act Two begins. We are ushered into Hades, the realm of departed spirits, in the unseen world beyond the grave. Again the contrasts startle us. Insight from the Hebrew beliefs about the afterlife help us to understand. Paradise and Gehenna were both considered part of Hades. But a great gulf separated the comfort, serenity, and peace of Paradise from the torturous, burning fires of Gehenna. Paradise was called Abraham's bosom, a realm of blessed assurance with the patriarch and all the people who were experiencing the reward of beatific bliss. Gehenna, like the burning refuse heap outside of Jerusalem, which burned but was never consumed, was a place of eternal torment in the flames of punishment.

We look closely. Jesus draws the veil and shows us Lazarus in Paradise and Dives in the fires of Gehenna. "Justice at last!" we say to ourselves. We watch Dives' anguish. Exactly what he had coming, we reflect. Our indignation over his blatant neglect of human need during his life subsides a bit as we watch Lazarus enjoying the peace and comfort that life never afforded him here. An uneasiness begins to grow in us, however, as we wonder what implications for us the Lord will draw from this pitiful picture. We are relieved when Act Two draws to a close.

Act 3

The scenery has not changed, however, as the final act begins. Our attention is riveted on Dives. He realizes where he is and that his condition in the eternal fires is irrevocable. Now he has no power to order underlings to satisfy his every whim and desire. The plight of his condition is intensified by his being able to see beyond the wide, yawning gulf between the fires of Gehenna and the solemnity of Paradise. He sees Lazarus reclining in Abraham's bosom. There are no leprous sores on his body; his face no longer has the pallid, tortured look of hunger. Joy radiates about him like a jewel in the sunshine.

We hear the screech and wrench in Dives' voice as he calls across the great divide. "Father Abraham, have mercy on me, and send Lazarus, that he may dip the tip of his finger in water and cool off my tongue; for I am in agony in this flame" (Luke 16:24, NASB). Dives is still giving orders. Imperious and indulgent of self even in hell. Strange twist of destiny: He had thrown bread crumbs out of his window for Lazarus to fight for with the wild alley dogs; now he wanted the liberated leper to cool his fevered tongue.

There is tenderness and unwavering firmness in Abraham's response across the abyss. "Child, remember that during your life you received your good things, and likewise Lazarus bad things; but now he is being comforted here, and you are in agony" (v. 25, NASB).

Abraham's words flash like lightning in Dives' soul. The thunder that followed was even more devastating to him. "And besides all this, between us and you there is a great chasm fixed, in order that those who wish to come over from here to you may not be able, and that none may cross over from there to us" (v. 26, NASB).

We wait in breathless anticipation for Dives' response. There is nothing for him to do but remember and regret. As the relentless flames leap about him, the corridors of his mind are occupied by the first selfless thought he has ever entertained. His five brothers. "Then I beg you, Father, that you send him to my father's house—for I have five brothers —that he may warn them, lest they also come to this place of torment" (vv. 27-28, NASB).

Abraham's answer is incisive: "They have Moses and the Prophets; let them hear them" (v. 29, NASB). The Law clearly revealed the ethical life, and the prophets had sounded a clarion call for justice, faithfulness, and obedience.

Dives persists: "No, Father Abraham, but if someone goes to them from the dead, they will repent!" (v. 30, NASB). Our hearts respond to Dives' plea. We are pulled with pity, strangely siding with this one we observed with angry consternation two acts before. Yes, Abraham, send someone! Warn the people.

Abraham's words in response echo with the authority of the majesty and awesomeness of God. "If they do not listen to Moses and the Prophets, neither will they be persuaded if someone rises from the dead" (v. 31, NASB).

The Message

The curtain closes slowly on the final act as Abraham speaks. We sit motionless. Catatonic. Stunned. What does it all mean? The Lord has drawn aside the thick, mysterious veil that stands between the here and now, and the then and forever after. It has forced us to see not only what is beyond this life but the inseparable link between life as we live it now, and how we will spend eternity. The truths mount in ascending power and resound in our souls.

1. The first is too good to be true, and yet too true to be taken lightly. Jesus has clearly told us that we will all live forever. Immortality is not our choice. Death is not an ending but a transition in immortal life. When our physical existence ends, we will live on in spirit. Our souls—the life composite of intellect, emotion, and will—are impervious to the power of death. That is both awesome and frightening, the basis of our hope and our deepest anxiety. All fears have their root in the ultimate fear of dying. The question lurks: Where will we spend eternity?

2. The second truth of the parable follows the first with disturbing clarity. There are two distinct realms of life after death. The Hebrews of Jesus' time had appropriate images that pervade the parable. We have Jesus' total message and the undeniable convictions of the New Testament. Jesus left no room for evasive equivocation about the reality of heaven or hell after death. In the Sermon on the Mount, He admonished, "But lay up for yourselves treasures in heaven, where neither moth nor rust destroys, and where thieves do not break in or steal; for where your treasure is, there will your heart be also" (Matthew 6:20-21, NASB). He came proclaiming the kingdom of heaven, and called people to begin a relationship with God that death could not end. His prayers were to "Our Father who art in heaven" (v. 9, NASB). Our ultimate reward was to be in heaven, and the Lord assured His disciples, "Let not your heart be troubled; believe in God, believe also in Me. In My Father's house are many dwelling places; if it were not so, I would have told you; for I go to prepare a place for you. And if I go and prepare a place for you, I will come again, and receive you to Myself; that where I am, there you may be also" (John 14:1-3, NASB). On the Cross, our Lord asserted His authority and promised the penitent thief that he would be with Him in Paradise.

But Christ's teaching about hell was no less vivid. He spoke of the "fire of hell" (Matthew 5:22) and the danger of being "cast into hell" (Mark 9:45, NASB). People were stunned by His directness about Satan's beguiling power to distort their potential for heaven, even though God's power is greater. "And do not fear those who kill the body, but are unable to kill the soul; but rather fear Him who is able to destroy both soul and body in hell" (Matthew 10:28, NASB).

Clearly, Jesus Christ came to liberate people from the power of Satan and the punishment of hell. Hell is eternal separation from God and all the resources of His love and forgiveness. The Lord came into our fallen creation to save sinners. He put it incisively so that there would be no doubt. "For God so loved the world, that He gave His only begotten Son, that whoever believes in Him should not perish, but have eternal life" (John 3:16, NASB). The abundant life He lived and offered to those who followed Him was not only for this side of the grave but forever.

3. That moves us on to the third truth of the parable. What we believe, and what we do about what we believe, determines our eternal destiny. Lazarus did not go to Abraham's bosom because he had been poor, nor Dives to hell fires because he was rich. Dives' destiny was sealed by the gulf that existed in his soul long before he died. The parable teaches us that we will continue in eternity in the spiritual condition in which we have spent the years of our life on earth. We assume Dives was a Hebrew. As such, he neglected not only the rites and rituals of his religion but also the basic requirements of the Law and the Prophets about care for the poor and needy. He was so completely centered on himself and his possessions that he no longer even saw Lazarus at his gate.

4. The pulse of Jesus' message quickens with the fourth penetrating point of the parable. Our Lord exposes the impotence of death. It is absolutely incapable of destroying the inner person. Dives and Lazarus were alive in Gehenna and Paradise immediately after death. Death did not destroy consciousness, memory, or self-identity. Dives knew himself to be Dives devoid of all his accumulation. He had the anguishing legacy of remembering what he had been and failed to do. There was no escape.

We know the grief of life's might-have-beens or the if-onlys. But on this side of the grave there is always the hope that we can do or say something to change the regrets of life. Death dashes that hope forever. We will have to live with the person we have become. Dives is the pitiful portrait of the excruciation of the unchangeable, immortal condition.

5. The final thing the parable teaches us is that the demarcation line of death is final, and there can be no communication with those on this side of the grave. There have been claims of mysterious manifestations and communications from the dead in dreams and through mediums. These are not enabled by the Holy Spirit but, if at all, by the evil one.

There is only one voice from the dead. His name is Jesus. He alone has come back. His voice is like "the sound of a trumpet" (Revelation 1:10, NASB), and like the "sound of many waters" (v. 15, NASB). He speaks with undeniable, irresistible clarity. "Do not be afraid; I am the first and the last, and the living One; and I was dead, and behold, I am alive forevermore, and I have the keys of death and of Hades" (vv. 17-18, NASB).

Abraham's words to Dives, that the living would not listen if someone rises from the dead, are both true and false. Many did not respond to the resurrected Lord when He returned as the Vanquisher of death. But many did. They became participants in what history called "the colony of the resurrection." For them death had lost its sting because it had no power to destroy the eternal life of their souls; the grave had no victory because it interred only the frail body from which the living spirits of the saints rose at the moment of physical demise.

The unconquerable charter of the Church was written in the red blood of Calvary and sealed with an empty tomb: "I am the resurrection and the life; he who believes in Me shall live even if he dies, and everyone who lives and believes in Me shall never die" (John 11:25-26, NASB).

Chapter 8

... Hypocrisy

by Jerry Hull

Background Scripture: Matthew 6:1-18; 23:27-28; Luke 6:41-45; 18:9-14

HYPOCRISY, *phoniness, pretense, sham, fake.* These are fighting words. Anger can explode in a fireball when we hang these words on a friend or work associate. None of us wants to be regarded as inauthentic. We want others to see us as real.

Jesus spoke harshly about hypocrisy. He hated phony pretense far more than we give Him credit for.

In fact, from the words and actions of Jesus, we can put together a "how to" manual on becoming a genuine, card-carrying hypocrite. This manual, inspired by the teachings of Christ, is built around these three tips on how to become a hypocrite:

1. Deceive with dishonest speech.
2. Pretend to be something you ain't.
3. Worship for show, not for God's praise.

Deceive with Dishonest Speech

This tip emerges from Matthew 5:37. Right in the middle of the Sermon on the Mount, Jesus offered this direction: "But let your statement be, 'Yes, yes' or 'No, no'; and anything beyond these is of evil" (NASB).

We down-home, ordinary people often complain, "Say what you mean. Mean what you say." Double-talk and elusive speeches troubled Jesus more than it does us. Carefully chosen words can mask, mislead, and distort. Unfortunately, schoolchildren, bureaucrats, spouses, and businessmen are all capable of this kind of "lying through their teeth," as we called it back on the farm.

I remember reading in Don Richardson's _Peace Child_ about his efforts to minister to the Sawi people of the former Netherlands New Guinea, north of Australia. The Sawi culture revered treachery and deceit. These people would take great pleasure in deceiving an enemy into thinking they wanted to make friends. Then when they had the full confidence of this enemy, they would kill him.

I can't help but wonder if our culture is moving in that same direction. And I'm not the only one wondering that. Walt Harrington, of the _Washington Post,_ recently wrote for the paper an essay titled "Has Truth Gone Out of Style?"

In this provocative piece, Harrington observed that lying is an in topic for journalists and social scientists. Pollsters feed us survey questions about lying. Publishers feed us books on lying. And nearly everyone and his brother feeds us lies.

As a result, we don't know who to believe. We've been duped by one too many sincere-looking appliance salesmen, car salesmen, politicians, television evangelists, and co-workers.

To our world of lies and liars, as well as to His, Christ said, "Simply let your 'Yes' be 'Yes,' and your 'No,' 'No.'" But what did He mean by that?

Some religious people of Jesus' day spoke the way we sometimes did in grade school. Remember when you made a promise, then later said you didn't need to keep it because you had your fingers crossed?

People of Jesus' time said their promises were good only if they swore an oath in God's name. If they swore in the name of the Temple or by the hills that surrounded Jerusalem, they were not obligated to keep their word.

Jesus would have nothing to do with such sham. In essence, Jesus said to be totally candid; mean what you say. If you say yes, then mean it. If you say no, then mean it and make your word good.

White lies, lies of convenience, and opportunistic lapses in memory are off-limits for Jesus' followers. Straightforward honesty in speech may be out of step with our day. It may not always work to our advantage. But Jesus requires it.

So the first tip on how to become a hypocrite is to deceive with dishonest speech.

Pretend to Be Something You Ain't

Hypocrites are phoney baloney. In fact, the idea of pretending to be something we're not is part of the root meaning of the word "hypocrite." Greek and Roman actors wore masks and puffed-out garments that made them appear bigger than life. Some masks even had a built-in megaphone. The word "hypocrite" comes out of this setting.

A hypocrite, then, is one who assumes a role, pretending to be someone else. Jesus addresses pretense—pretending to be something we ain't. Look at Matthew 23:27-28 and Luke 6:41-45.

Jesus employed graphic words to expose pretense. He said, in the Matthew 23:27-28 passage, that the religious leaders of His day paraded about, pretending to be righteous. But in reality, Jesus declared, inside they were filled with dead men's bones and every other unclean thing you can imagine.

These two perceptions disagree by a country mile. Decayed bones, rotten garments, and rusty bits of metal are a far sight from the way a self-righteous preacher wishes to present himself. Jesus observed, "On the outside you appear to people as righteous but on the inside you are full of hypocrisy and wickedness" (v. 28).

In Luke 6 Jesus used different figures of speech. In verse 43 Jesus spoke of bad trees pretending to be good trees. In verse 44 our Lord referred to brier bushes pretending to be grapevines.

Pretense, pretending to be something you ain't, is eventually exposed. Jesus concluded His discussions about bad trees and brier bushes by saying, "The good man brings good things out of the good stored up in his heart, and the evil man brings evil things out of the evil stored up in his heart" (v. 45). In other words, if down in the roots a person is a brier bush, that person will produce brier barbs, not Concord grapes.

The point is clear: Righteousness is not achieved by simply deciding to be righteous. Sooner or later the brier bushes will be revealed for what they are, regardless of how we attempt to disguise ourselves as grapevines. Jesus challenges us to look deep inside and examine what's there.

Are we the real thing? Flocks of Canadian geese spend much of the winter in southwest Idaho. I enjoy watching them feed in fields near our house. From time to time, hunters scatter decoys in the field in an attempt to lure some geese in for a landing. These decoys are colorful, beautiful, and stately in their pose. They are pretenders, however. They are not geese at all—simply hard, plastic, lifeless imitations.

Sometimes we're like those plastic geese. We claim to be faithful husbands and yet flirt with work associates. We give a pretense of being trustworthy while helping ourselves to materials that belong to the company. We claim to be hardworking students while stealing through plagiarism. We claim to be responsible citizens while failing to report all our income for tax purposes. We claim to be loyal friends while gossiping about our friends' flaws.

Jesus called for us to allow God to change the inside to make it match the upright, decent persons we wish to appear to be.

We don't need to pretend to be righteous. Rather, we can allow Christ to live out His life through us. We can let the righteousness of Christ escape through our words, our actions, our relationships, our aspirations, our goals, our dreams, and our life-styles.

The second tip on how to be a hypocrite is to pretend to be something we ain't.

Worship for Show, Not for God's Praise

In Matthew 6:1 we read a warning. Jesus said, "Be careful not to do your 'acts of righteousness' before men, to be seen by them. If you do, you will have no reward from your Father in heaven."

Compare another passage. In Luke 18:14 Jesus made it plain and simple: "Everyone who exalts himself will be humbled, and he who humbles himself will be exalted."

From these two verses, and the contexts that surround each, we find a third tip on how to be a hypocrite. Any would-be hypocrite should worship for show, not for God's praise.

I suspect we modern Christians worship for show more than we realize. Let me illustrate. In your church, what kind of worker is hardest to find: someone to sing from the platform once a month, or someone to help out in the nursery once a month?

As another illustration, how many times have you showed up for worship services simply because of peer pressure or to impress someone—like parents, children, pastor, or friends? The wife of a pastor in a small, struggling church once said to a friend of mine that guilt is not always a bad motivation for coming to church. She wasn't talking about sin guilt. She was talking about the guilt we impose on our people for not being in church "whenever the doors are open." I can't help but wonder if this woman was doing a little rationalizing of the pressure she and her husband put on their people to attend church, pressure for attendance growth that pastors get put on them from district and general church leadership.

Our reasons for attending worship services should have nothing to do with how others view us. We should be there to praise God.

One more illustration of how we modern Christians sometimes worship for show is revealed on the bronze plaques posted in our churches. Are we more inclined to give money if we are guaranteed that our name will be engraved in bronze for generations to come?

In many denominations individuals occasionally donate to missions enough money to build a church overseas. Unfortunately, it is also common for these donors to insist that the church be named after them. But the "Jerry Hull Memorial Church" in Kenya would make as much sense as the "Nimbu Wassi Memorial Church" in Peoria.

In Matthew 6:1-18 Jesus identified the importance of motives. Here, Jesus revealed we can do the right things with the wrong motives, and in so doing, displease God.

In this way, worship becomes an act of hypocrisy. Let's hear Jesus on this point. "When you pray, do not be like the hypocrites, for they love to pray standing in the synagogues and on the street corners to be seen by men" (Matthew 6:5). The last phrase, "to be seen by men," reveals the key problem. Worship should be for the audience of one Person, God himself, not our peers. We are not to worship in order to be noticed by others.

When I was in second grade, I received a beautiful gift from my parents: a leather-bound New Testament that included the Book of Psalms. I treasured that gift. My parents taught me the value of reading out of the Bible each day. I followed their advice to read one chapter from the Bible each night before going to bed. I must confess that I sometimes searched for the shortest psalm I could find.

A couple of years later, I noticed an interesting thing at church. I noticed that the Bibles of the saintly people were frayed. I wanted my Bible to look like that. I planned a way to rush the process along. Instead of waiting for the wear to come from a decade of daily use, I rolled the corners of the leather covers up.

Such behavior is not acceptable even for a nine-year-old boy. And it certainly is inappropriate for teens and adults. Few of us roll up the corners of our Bibles, as I did. But how many of us engage in praying, giving, fasting, and other acts of worship primarily for appearance?

Showmanship in worship is stressed in a parable Jesus told. We find this parable in Luke 18:9-14. The two key actors, a Pharisee and a tax collector, were both engaged in prayer. The Pharisee posted himself at the busiest spot near the Temple. He prayed loudly so that all would hear and see him. The tax collector, in contrast, went to an out-of-the-way place, far from the crowd, and offered a contrite prayer of confession.

You don't need a doctorate in theology to understand Jesus' conclusion. Hypocrisy doesn't make the grade. Hypocrisy is despicable to others around us and nauseating to God.

We are social creatures and thus easily tempted in this manner of worshiping for show. I still struggle with this occasionally, especially when I'm called on to lead in public prayer. I have a graduate degree in theology and was ordained an elder 25 years ago. In spite of these credentials, leading in prayer is difficult.

Thoughts of others in the crowd press upon me. I wonder how I am perceived. And I'm tempted to want to appear learned and to display theological savvy.

In Matthew 6 Jesus revealed that in our worship we may, in fact, gain the favor and recognition of people. He added, however, that's all we'll get. Note verse 2, in which Jesus says that those who do things for show "have received their reward in full."

Though modeling, as an object lesson for the younger generation, requires constant attention, and though the next generation deserves conspicuous displays of righteous living, the reason for worship must primarily be a white-hot love for our Lord. Then everyone who sees our worship will know it is for His glory and not for show. Perhaps this is the context in which we understand Jesus' words when He told us that people will see our good deeds but will praise our Father in heaven (see Matthew 5:16).

Deceitful speech, pretense, and worship for show are surefire ways for achieving hypocrisy. These methods, however, place us in opposition to God. God wants us to live as transparent, honest people desiring to please Him. Authentic living for God's glory may not always find rewards in this life. But Jesus promised that our Father God sees and rewards people who are genuinely real.

Jerry Hull is professor of social work at Northwest Nazarene College, Nampa, Idaho.

Chapter 9

... Divorce
and Remarriage

by Al Truesdale

Background Scripture: Deuteronomy 24:1-4; Matthew 19:3-12

MARRIAGE was her ticket out of a diseased home. No longer would Robin* have to endure her father's sexual molesting. No more would she have to hide in corners of the house while her parents screamed at one another over the chronic money problems.

But Robin only traded one brand of torment for another. Now, six years into marriage, she is habitually abused by a husband whose best friend is alcohol. In spite of intense ridicule, Robin has become a Christian. And, when her husband allows it, she and the two children attend church.

Through an amazing display of determination and fortitude, Robin has completed training that qualifies her as a dietician. Now that she's able to support herself, she is thinking more and more about divorce.

Robin isn't the only Christian I know of who's considering divorce.

Bill and Maxine grew up in the same church, participated in its youth activities, attended the same Christian college, and dated almost no one else. In their senior year of college they were married to one another amid congratulations and great anticipation.

But, three years into marriage, Bill discovered his "lost teen and college years," and those missed rites of exploration and rebellion. The church became an object of blame for "pushing him into marriage." And at work he discovered Laura, who promised to help him "recover what he had missed."

Bill now lives with Laura, expresses no remorse, and vows never to return to Maxine, who lives in the twilight of confusion, guilt, and suspended social growth. For two years her days and nights have faded into an endless cycle of self-contempt and uncertainty. Though horrified by the thought of divorce, Maxine wonders whether the nightmare in which she lives is the future to which a forgiving and redeeming God would doom her.

Alter these two stories to fit a thousand different circumstances, and still someone will be waiting to present another tragedy.

One of the most unsettling realities of our time is the endless parade of marriages that marches out of the light of high expectations and into the night of maddening despair.

The Questions

What word of instruction does Christ give to the Robins and Maxines who increasingly populate our churches? Does the Bible even address situations such as these? Can Christ and His Church offer a word of forgiveness and hope, instruction and restoration? Or is the Church qualified only to apply a rigid rule that condemns and accents failure without providing any path toward restoration and starting over?

Can the Church do no more than play it safe by adhering to a high standard of marriage, and then ignore the agonizing facts of life that disrupt and destroy many marriages?

A Christian approach to the subject of divorce and remarriage has to make room for the entire message of Christ, both what He said about the Christian standard for marriage, *and* what He revealed about the kind of God He presented to the stream of personal failures in the Gospels.

What Jesus Said About
Divorce and Remarriage

The first three Gospels record four instances in which Jesus spoke of divorce and remarriage, twice in Matthew and once each in Mark and Luke. In two of these instances, what Jesus said resulted from a run-in with the Pharisees (Matthew 19:3-12; Mark 10:2-9). Always alert for opportunities to discredit Jesus, the Pharisees thought they had Him cornered. Jesus had preached God's forgiveness, and the Pharisees had seen Him freely extend forgiveness to sinners. Christ had spoken and acted as though God would forgive anything. And He had taught that those who obey God must be as forgiving in their relationships with others.

The Pharisees also knew that the Law of Moses allowed or even required divorce for certain offenses. Forgiveness didn't even enter the picture. Clearly, it seemed to the Pharisees, Jesus would be in conflict with the Law if He were to make forgiveness the standard in marriage and exclude divorce.

"Teacher," the Pharisees asked, "when is it all right for a man to divorce his wife?" Now the Pharisees didn't doubt that divorce was permitted; they just argued over when it could occur. In fact, there were two main schools of thought on the matter. One was the liberal school, identified with Rabbi Hillel (HILL-el), which allowed divorce for even the most trivial offenses, as, for example, when a wife spoke disrespectfully of him. The other school, identified with Rabbi Shammai (SHAM-mi), believed that adultery was the only justifiable reason for divorce.

Both schools thought they were faithfully interpreting the Law of Moses as stated in Deuteronomy 24:1-4. Divorce, they were certain, was provided for by God. They were technically correct. In order to divorce a wife, a husband was supposed to lodge a bill of divorce against her if she were to commit "some indecency" (Deuteronomy 24:1, RSV). Uncertainty about the meaning of "some indecency" sparked disagreements that led to the different interpretations by Rabbi Hillel and Rabbi Shammai.

To the surprise of both the Pharisees and Jesus' disciples, Christ rejected both interpretations. He said, "All of you are wrong." According to Jesus, Moses made an allowance for divorce *only* because of the hardness of heart exhibited by husbands who acted selfishly or who were unwilling to forgive a wife's offenses (Matthew 19:8; Mark 10:5). These hard-hearted husbands rejected God's original plan for marriage.

According to Jesus, in marriage God creates a new reality that offenses ought not dissolve. Forgiveness and reconciliation—even reconciliation after adultery—are supposed to be the pattern for marriage. So Jesus attached an importance and permanency to marriage that shocked the Pharisees and the disciples (Matthew 19:10).

When we look closely at what He taught regarding marriage, we see it is totally consistent with the gospel He preached and the God He revealed. The story of the prodigal

son, Christ's acceptance of sinners, His acceptance of Zacchaeus into the kingdom of God, forgiveness of the woman
taken in adultery, and most importantly, His death on the
Cross, revealed a God who longs for reconciliation between
himself and His estranged creation.

Christ's response to the Pharisees about divorce is an
excellent expression of how He thought we should extend
God's grace to others, especially in marriage. For those who
follow the gospel of Jesus Christ in all of life's relationships,
including marriage, there are no exceptions to forgiveness.

However, Jesus said something to the Pharisees that
seems to allow for divorce in one exceptional situation. In
two instances in Matthew, Jesus seems to say that adultery
is a legitimate cause for divorce: "But I say to you that every
one who divorces his wife, except on the ground of unchastity, makes her an adulteress" (5:32, RSV). Apparently
Jesus recognized that when an adulterous betrayal occurs,
the foundations for marriage can dissolve. In this instance,
He seems to say that forgiveness and reconciliation are not
required.

However, as surprising as it might be, we simply do not
know for certain the meaning of the Greek word translated
as "unchastity." Some scholars say Jesus meant to name
adultery as an exception to His prohibition against divorce.
Others think Jesus meant that if an engaged woman proved
unfaithful during the time of engagement, the man to whom
she was engaged could "divorce her" (Matthew 1:19, RSV).

Dissatisfied with these interpretations, other scholars
maintain that the "except clause" refers to incestuous marriages that were forbidden by the Law of Moses (Leviticus
18:6-18). Since such marriages were illegitimate, to dissolve
such a "marriage" would be not only permissible but even
demanded.

Still other scholars reject all three of these interpretations. They say the "except clause" was never spoken by
Jesus, and that it was added later to apply the teachings of

Jesus to a problem regarding illegal incestuous marriages. Faced with an illicit marriage by one or more converts, the early Christians, or Matthew himself, simply added the words they believed Jesus would have spoken concerning this subject. Given the sanctity Jesus attached to marriage, incestuous marriages were judged to be dissolvable.

Why is there so much disagreement over a phrase that seems to be clear? The main problem, as I've mentioned, is that no one knows for certain the meaning of the Greek word for "unchastity" in Matthew 5:32 and 19:9. In the first century this word, *porneia* (por-NAY-a), could refer to almost any form of sexual immorality. It included adultery but was not limited to that. By contrast, the second word used in the last part of the verses, *moikeia* (moi-KAY-a), meant *only* adultery.

If Jesus had meant to name adultery as the one exception under which divorce and remarriage are permissible for Christians, why, the scholars ask, did Matthew not use the same Greek word in both parts of the verse? Furthermore, why do the "except clauses" seem to contradict what Jesus said about divorce in Mark (10:2-12) and Luke (16:18), where no acceptable conditions for divorce are given?

For these reasons, a growing number of scholars are discounting the idea that Jesus identified adultery as a legitimate reason for divorce. When we combine Jesus' specific statements regarding divorce with the difficult problems associated with the meaning of *porneia*, and with the distinguishing features of the gospel He preached, it seems clear that He believed marriage was intended for a lifetime. Furthermore, in Matthew, Mark, and Luke the Lord condemns remarriage as adulterous.

So, for Jesus, marriage was to reflect the new reality of the gospel itself—covenant, forgiveness, reconciliation, unconditional love, and growth in unity.

What About the Robins and Maxines?

If all this is true, how are we to respond to Robin and Maxine? What does Christ have to say to those Christians whose marriages have hopelessly collapsed, either before they became Christians or afterward?

As in all moral crises, we must ask, "Which course of action is most faithful to the gospel of Jesus Christ?" And as with many moral questions, the answers are not always immediately clear.

When we consider the way Jesus dealt with the tragedies of life, it is clear that faithfulness to His gospel demands that we take seriously the tragic and complex factors present in failed marriages. This is part of what makes the gospel good news. It offers hope, forgiveness, and restoration in situations that are filled with failure, guilt, fear, and despair. The gospel does not address successful situations only. It speaks in the presence of failures as well. For the gospel to be God's good news, it must be good news in bad times too.

How can we help the Robins and Maxines hear good news and not simply a new pharisaism that drives them deeper into despair?

First, let's look at what we must not do. In the interest of being merciful and redemptive we must not downplay the Christian standard for marriage. It must be extolled, pursued, taught to our children, and celebrated as a sacrament of God's grace.

Next, we must not whittle away at the New Testament until we succeed in making Jesus' teachings comply with our situation. Let Jesus' teaching stand as it is. In it we learn the power and meaning of the gospel as it relates to marriage.

But finally, we cannot think we have served the gospel well simply by condemning failures—by telling people, "This is the way it should have been." If we take that path, then all of us will be excluded.

Second, let's look at what we can do. Marriage is a covenant in which two people promise to give themselves totally to each other. This should occur in God's power and in responsibility before Him.

Often, however, people who are now Christians were married and divorced, and perhaps subsequently remarried, before they became Christians. They neither advocated nor followed a Christian standard of marriage. They made decisions, experienced failures, and took actions that shattered their marriages.

But through the marvelous grace of God these people encountered the Christ who takes the broken pieces of life and makes all things new. The Epistles of the New Testament show this happening repeatedly in the pagan world of the first century. At no point do we hear the apostle Paul saying, "Because of your past scars—your participation in idol worship and temple prostitution—you must forever live with a limited and crippled form of Christian discipleship. You must always have hanging over your heads the guilt that your past sins and failures produced."

No! It was to former prostitutes and pagans that the apostle Paul said, "If anyone is in Christ, he is a new creation; the old has gone, the new has come!" (2 Corinthians 5:17).

Although memories of past failures cannot be erased, and continuing responsibilities must be fulfilled, it is a violation of the New Testament to freeze a person into his past. The Samaritan woman to whom Jesus promised the water of life could not go back and correct her past. Nevertheless, Christ promised to her the water of life.

"But," someone says, "not all marital failures occur before one becomes a Christian." Furthermore, "There are people who are Christians but who live in abusive and in other kinds of destructive marital circumstances. What hope can Christ give to them?"

More and more conservative scholars are listening to the full message of Christ, then concluding that there are circumstances that are sufficiently destructive, either emotionally, psychologically, or physically, to call for separation, and even divorce. Too often, in our sincere desire to uphold the Christian standard of marriage, we have been insensitive to the catastrophic marital circumstances in which some people live.

This is not offered as an escape clause to release a person from committed efforts to make a marriage succeed. But it recognizes the truth that nowhere in the Gospels does Christ impose a harsh code that requires a person to endure his own gradual destruction at the hands of the other person who once promised to be a covenantal partner.

The scholars who acknowledge this believe it is a miscarriage of the gospel and the cruelest expression of legalism to tell a person who is caught in a catastrophic marriage, "According to Jesus, you must remain married, no matter what threats the marriage presents." This teaching recognizes that the marriage covenant can be so recklessly and repeatedly violated that all bases of marriage disappear. And it recognizes that the newness of life given in Christ makes possible deliverance from such chaos, forgiveness for sins, and the grace to start again.

The apostle Paul recognized this. In 1 Corinthians 7:15 he writes that a Christian woman should no longer feel bound to an unbelieving husband who has abandoned her.

Let us consider an even more difficult problem. What about those marital failures among Christians that are marked not by physical or severe emotional abuse but by intense alienation, isolation, and simmering contempt? Most troubled Christian marriages can be healed if the appropriate resources are identified and used.

Many divorces occur among Christians because they lack the discipline, maturity, and love necessary for a successful marriage. But what about those instances in which reconciliation is simply an impossibility, where marriage has become so mutually destructive that it squeezes the emotional and religious life out of both parties? The basis for marriage has broken apart like Humpty Dumpty, "and all the king's horses, and all the king's men . . ."

Foolish is the person who unhesitatingly advises all such people to get a divorce. But more and more conservative students of the Bible are saying that equally unwise is the one who insists that never in such situations should divorce be considered.

Joyce married a young man who was preparing to be a minister. In the succeeding months she discovered the painful truth that her husband could not successfully pursue any goal, was lazy to the point of being unwilling to care for her, and appeared to have strong homosexual tendencies.

Joyce felt she had made a horrible mistake. She eventually divorced the man who showed no signs of wanting to be a husband.

Today she is married to a man who has a unique and effective Christian ministry. Both are active members of their church, and they give every indication of being happily married. Did Joyce make the correct decision, or should she have "stuck it out" the rest of her life?

A Final Reminder

In the pagan environment in which we live, divorce has become an epidemic. But the New Testament proclaims that we can live godly lives in spite of our pagan environment. And the Word reminds us that marriage and the home are included, not excluded, from the enabling power of the Holy Spirit.

But we must be careful not to allow this holy standard to become a new legalism that beats down those who have failed. Had the gospel Jesus preached provided hope only for the successful person, there would have been no story of Zacchaeus, Mary Magdalene, or the woman at the well. Neither would your name or mine appear in the Book of Life.

*The names and some of the situations in this chapter have been changed.

Al Truesdale is professor of Christian ethics at Nazarene Theological Seminary, Kansas City.

Chapter 10

... the New Birth

by Nina Beegle

Background Scripture: John 3:1-17; Luke 8:4-15; 18:15-17

I WAS DESPERATELY passing out the oxygen equipment-of-the-day to the 48 passengers on the DC-4 as the plane climbed to the 15,000-foot limit that the Civil Aeronautics Administration had placed on commercial airliners. The air gets pretty thin up there, and pressurized cabins on airlines were available only on the new DC-6s.

Some of the passengers were already unconscious. I fitted oxygen masks over their faces, covered them with blankets, and did all the things airline hostesses were instructed to do in such emergencies.

Still the unscheduled storm was tossing the plane about like a crumb in a cracker box. Over the intercom, the pilot instructed the junior stewardess and me to buckle into our "jump seats" as soon as possible and get some oxygen for ourselves.

Lightning seemed to flash down the aisle of the plane and along its wings, giving the appearance of a plane on fire. The engines spit and sputtered as we were dumped and swooped by giant updrafts and downdrafts.

Ordinarily my adventuresome spirit reveled in the excitement and activity of a storm, but this one had me scared. I wasn't sure whether I was seeing atmospheric activity or engines on fire, but one thing I was sure of as I contemplated my fate. If this plane crashed before it got to Denver, I was on my way to hell. How I knew that so certainly is still something of a mystery to me, because about all I had opportunity to know of hell was that it was a word people used when they were angry. But that night I felt I was being dangled over it, and it was a place I didn't want to go.

No preacher had explained heaven or hell to me, for church wasn't included in our family's life-style as we grew up. I had never heard John 3:16, nor "Jesus loves me! this I know, / For the Bible tells me so." But in that hour I promised God that if He'd get that plane to Denver, "I'll do anything You want me to do. I'll go anywhere You want me to go. I'll say anything You want me to say, and be anything You want me to be."

I walked off the plane in Denver, glad to be alive, and with an inexplicable sense that nothing would ever be the same again. In the dispatch office everyone was babbling about the unexpected, previously undetected storm and what had happened to other planes. A Braniff DC-3, they said, had flipped completely over.

"How was your trip?" someone asked me.

"Oh, peachy. Just peachy," I quipped, too tired to discuss it.

The next morning I awoke and sat up in bed. The other gals had left me alone in the hotel suite. Something was different. I felt as though a light had been turned on inside me. I sat there in awe—wondering why I felt so good, so luxuriously happy, like never before. The promises I made to God in the plane walked across my consciousness: "I will *do . . . go . . . say . . . be.*" I really meant them.

I couldn't have explained to anyone why, overnight, my desires had changed, my motives had changed, *everything* had changed. I would later learn from God's Word that I had been "born again," as Jesus explained it to Nicodemus in the Gospel of John, chapter 3. I still get goosebumps when I tell this story, though it happened many years ago.

The Mystery of the New Birth

Jesus said, "I tell you the truth, no one can see the kingdom of God unless he is born again" (John 3:3).

What is this mystery called the "new birth" that comes unseen, incomprehensibly, like the wind, and forever changes the course of one's life? "You must be born again," Jesus said. "The wind blows wherever it pleases. You hear its sound, but you cannot tell where it comes from or where it is going. So it is with everyone born of the Spirit" (vv. 7-8).

No one has ever caught a piece of the wind in the hand to examine it, yet its evidence is unmistakable and real. We can see leaves flutter, but that is not the wind. We can catch the exhilarating aroma of new-mown grass or freshly baked bread, but that is not the wind, for it has no odor of its own. It is so strong it can uproot a giant tree by its long-entrenched roots, or it can gently lift a lock of hair. It is a mystery—something we must believe in, though we cannot see it or handle it.

Why did I accept the gentle, refreshing wind of the Spirit while others rejected it?

Jesus said it was a matter of soil (Luke 8:4-15).

The soil of the heart can be prepared by inside and outside forces. It can become parched, rocky, or fertile soil, depending on the response of its owner to the outside and inside forces.

Tracy* was a teenager in a church my husband pastored. This young lady hardened her heart in response to conditions in her home. Why should she believe the Word of God she heard in church when it never changed her parents?

As things got more tense at home, and hate and bickering seemed to bounce off the walls, Tracy laid her own plans. One night she did not come home. After 24 hours the police were notified. They soon learned she had been seen with two young men, driving across the state line. Tracy was only 16, so it became a case for the FBI. Tracy was found and returned to her home, but the "gospel-hardened" girl eventually went the whole route with drugs, then pregnancy, then high school dropout. She had neither the ears to hear nor the heart to receive what she heard in Sunday School and church. The soil had not been properly prepared.

I lost track of Tracy, and I don't know whether the good seed ever found fertile soil in her heart.

Jesus said we must have the right kind of ears (Luke 8:18; 14:35; John 6:45). Jesus knew His words would not get to the hearts of some because they wouldn't let His truth enter their ears. Some people have ears that receive the truth, while others tune it out so that it can't be programmed into their thinking. They become spiritually deaf. But Jesus told Pilate, "Everyone on the side of truth *listens* to me" (John 18:37, italics added). Therefore when He explained the parable of the soil and the seed, He said, "He who has ears to hear, let him hear" (Luke 8:8).

The human will is involved in any spiritual decision or choice, and that is what determines the listening or the turning of a deaf ear.

Like a Child

Jesus declared, "Anyone who will not receive the kingdom of God like a little child will never enter it" (Luke 18:17).

Jesus had just told the story of the tax collector who humbly approached God, beat on his chest, and said, "God be merciful to me a sinner" (v. 13, KJV), and the Pharisee who came in pride and self-righteousness to declare how good he was.

As if that were not enough of a lesson on humility, the people began "bringing babies to Jesus," and He told all those grown-ups that they could not get into heaven unless they became like these babies.

That is the reason new birth in Christ does not appeal to many. It cuts across the pride of self-sufficiency, position, wealth, personal appearance, and reputation. And it puts us in a position of utter dependency on God as a baby is upon his parents. But that is not the end of Jesus' comparison.

At birth, a baby comes out of the darkness of the womb into the light of the sun. In spiritual birth it is the same: The soul comes out of the darkness of sin into the light of the Son.

What, then, is the first thing we expect from the new baby? We all listen intently. If he does not make a sound, we are alarmed. For he could be stillborn—dead! Otherwise, he proclaims his existence in the most profound terms. Likewise the spiritually newborn cannot be silent about the great phenomenon of life he has experienced.

Next, the newborn thirsts for milk, and again the analogy continues. The "newborn babes" thirst for the "sincere milk of the word" (1 Peter 2:2, KJV). Without it he will die.

The innocent child looks to its parents trustingly and receives their teaching. He is not looking at truth from a position of guilt or prejudice as adults so often do.

Renae and David are a young couple I have counseled. One evening, in front of their son, they had a disagreement that got out of hand. David said some harsh things, and when the little family sat down to dinner, the atmosphere was tense. Renae picked at her food.

"Renae, I'm sorry I said those things," said David. "Will you forgive me?"

"That's what you always do," Renae pouted. "You always get mad and say mean things and then say you're sorry. Well, sometimes sorry *just doesn't cut it!*"

Silence reigned for a moment, then six-year-old Kent said, "But, Mom, we learned in Sunday School that sorry *should* cut it. The Bible says if somebody asks us to forgive them, we should forgive them."

Kent's parents had instilled in him that the Bible was truth. Because he trusted his parents' teaching, he accepted that unequivocally and was used of God to bring reconciliation around the dinner table that evening.

The analogy of the physical birth and the spiritual birth breaks down at one point: choice. Spiritual rebirth involves our will and requires that we choose to be born into God's family.

A Christian family cannot bring us into spiritual birth. Our denomination or religious affiliation, though we be fourth-generation "Church of Perfect Love," cannot make us children of God. We are born of God in that moment of divine revelation in which the Holy Spirit brings us to a decision.

A Guilty Heart on the Run

Jesus said He did not come to condemn the world but to save it (John 3:16-17).

The guilty heart runs from God. David S. McCarthy, in *That Unforgettable Encounter,* tells of an incident in an adult Sunday School class.

"One Sunday we dealt with an encounter between Jesus and one of His followers. Multiple-choice questions were printed on the chalkboard, and students were asked to choose one answer to the following statement:

"If Jesus met me today, He would probably:

a. Chew me out.

b. Give me a swift kick in the pants.

c. Put His arms around me and hug me.

d. Ask if I wanted Him to make me whole.

"Nearly all the students selected *a* or *b.* They felt threatened by an encounter with Jesus and saw the event mostly in negative terms."

Jesus invites us to come to Him, not as a condemning judge, but as a loving Savior. Such magnetic love, it would seem, would override guilt. But for some it takes a lot of patient teaching—yes, and loving.

Pam, a good friend of mine, was in and out and up and down in her spiritual life, though she was raised in a Christian home and had gone to church most of her life. There was no doubt about her sincerity or her commitment to Jesus, at least not from the church folk who observed her life. She was a humble, open person, beautiful in spirit. But she felt she did not have the continuous flow of joy that should have accompanied the new birth and consequent devotion to God.

More often than not, the preaching of the Word seemed to bring condemnation to her heart rather than encouragement. One Sunday, I knelt at the altar to pray with her about this. She could not seem to put her finger on anything amiss in her spiritual walk. She seemed penitent, and I felt certain if there *was* something, God himself would surely put *His* finger on it.

I later learned that as she grew up, she felt unaccepted by her father. Whether it was simply a lack of affirmation and praise on his part, or unreasonable criticism, I do not know. But this family history seemed to play a part in Pam's long struggle to finally rest in God's accepting love without any feeling of condemnation.

Pam had to learn that the new birth means she was a new creature, accepted by Jesus just as she was—past sins forgiven, but a spiritual baby ready to grow and develop as one of God's children.

We began this chapter with the mystery of the Holy Spirit moving like the wind to bring awareness and revelation to the heart. In the new birth He brings Christ—the knowledge of Him and the presence of Him. Let's conclude with the great mystery of His continuing work in the human heart and life.

Now He sets us apart for God and for one another. He empowers us for service. The mystery of God at work in our lives takes us along our spiritual journey from birth to maturity, and into eternity.

The kingdom of God will be perpetuated only as we, by an act of love, bear new spiritual children. They "must be born again," and our responsibility after that becomes that of parents, nurturing and loving them to maturity.

We are to be perpetuators of new birth and new life, for we are the children of the Author of Life.

*Names have been changed, but the people are real, and the events took place as described.

Nina Beegle is a free-lance writer and formerly the editor for the Division of Church Growth at the Church of the Nazarene Headquarters. She is the wife of a Free Methodist pastor in Canon City, Colo.

Chapter 11

"Miss Finley, find out what Harrison has to smile about!"

. . . Holy Living

by Reuben R. Welch

Background Scripture: John 17:9-19

MANY OF US have developed the "if only" syndrome. We feel that "if only things were different," we could serve Christ more faithfully.

Often I have thought, If only my house were arranged differently, I could be a better Christian. My house has a den connected to the living room, with a sliding glass door between. The living room is where we have good light and comfortable chairs where I can sit and read the Bible and meditate and . . . be holy. But the trouble is, just a few feet away in the den is the television set. It's hard for me to be holy in the living room, when out of the corner of my eye, I can see the television and hear things that sound so interesting. I don't like television, of course; but on occasion I look up just in time to see some dastardly deed done to a fellow primate. And I say, "Well, how come that?" So an hour and 47 commercials later, I'm not as holy as I was before. So you see, my house is just not set up for me to be holy in.

I could be more holy if I didn't have to drive the freeway to work. I'm not kidding! Day after day, I set out from home to go and be a blessing to my students at school; and by the time I get there, I'm the one who needs prayer. I leave home at a quarter of seven in the morning, and the freeway is already full of dumbhead people who crowd the lanes and give stupid signals! You understand what I'm saying, don't you?

I am sure you could be more holy if only you had a different roommate, if you had a better car (or even a car), if you had a different job, if your spouse were different, if your house were different . . . if . . . if . . . if . . .

Home, family, TV, work, people, the car—these are the things of my common, daily life! I have begun to see that the "if only" syndrome leads to a rejection of the created world, a turning away from God's order.

Jesus said, "They are in the world . . . I do not pray that thou shouldst take them out of the world, but that thou shouldst keep them from the evil one" (John 17:11, 15, RSV). I believe that God's will for us is not so much to be separated from the things of the world as to be separated from our own false selves—set free to live in His world and use His "things" for His glory.

My responsibilities take me out of town from time to time. And I have reasonable assurance, based on the law of averages, that something will go wrong at home while I am away. Some part of my car will need to be repaired. My office will be piled higher with mail and stuff that needs to be done. But whatever goes wrong, this is still my world. And I hear Jesus saying that He has given me everything He has promised in this world where I live. Granted, the life I live in the Lord is indeed a life of tension; the tension is found in the two statements: "They are thine"; and, "They are in the world" (John 17:9, 11, RSV). Christian disciples belong to God, but they are in the world. We have not fully realized the ambivalent character of living "between the times." We live between the time of birth and death, the first and second coming, the time of our entering into life in Christ and being made perfect in Him in glory. Yet amid the tensions that are part of our human existence, we belong to God, and our participation is in the world. We ought to recognize that it is not a simple thing to be an obedient disciple in the world.

What does it mean to be in the world, yet not of it? Let me gather some verses from the 17th chapter of John that point us toward an answer: "Sanctify them in the truth; thy word is truth. As thou didst send me into the world, so I have sent them into the world. And for their sake I consecrate myself, that they also may be consecrated in truth" (vv. 17-19, RSV). Jesus' prayer for His in-the-world Church is that it be holy; His heart's desire for us real-world people is that we be holy. If we want to understand what He expects of us, we must grapple with the meaning of the word *holy*.

The Meaning of *Holy*

What does Jesus mean when He prays for us to be made holy? At the end of the Bible studies and the journal articles and the textbook examinations, it seems to me that one great idea emerges: *To be holy means to be different by virtue of belonging to God.* The first important word to notice in that sentence is *belonging.* Only God is holy. Other things or persons become holy by virtue of their relationship with God. That is why the Israelite Temple, along with its vestments and ceremonial utensils, could be considered holy; all of those things belonged uniquely to God. Then what must we say of holy *people?* Fundamentally, the Bible says that people likewise are holy because they belong to God. So when Jesus prays that we become holy, He is asking that our wills and intentions be entirely devoted to God and to His service. All of our talents, all of our energies, indeed our lives in their entirety, should be marked with the seal of consecration. The seal of consecration implies a renouncing of self, just as Jesus was willing to renounce all of His heavenly claims in order to serve His Father on earth. That is a radical belonging to God.

When we realize that God is holy, we understand why we need cleansing and a liberation from the power of the carnal mind in the process of moving into a holy relationship with Him. If we are to belong to the community that belongs to God, we need the cleansing and empowering of His Holy Spirit. I am hearing the words of an old invitation hymn:

> Break down every idol,
> Cast out every foe.
> —JAMES NICHOLSON

As the Word of God penetrates my life, I find that it has increasing power and magnetism; it makes expanding demands upon me; and it speaks reassuringly about who I am—a Christ person.

The second important word in our definition of holiness is *different*. We become different by belonging to God. As it was with the old Israel, so with the new Israel. Old Israel was different from the surrounding nations because every part of their life was related to God. The Israelite people were to reflect God's character and will as spelled out in the Book of the Covenant. For us of the new covenant, the same dynamics apply. Our radical belonging to God results in lives that reflect God's character and will.

What does that mean for me personally? It means that I am to live in growing likeness to Jesus through the power of His Spirit.

We are in the world, sent to the world. And if we are going to be persons who put God at the center of our lives and proclaim God to the world, we must do it with the rooms of our homes arranged as they are. We may have to learn to like our cars the way they are. We may need to accept the intrusion of people around us to whom we want to shout, "Would you please leave me alone so that I can be holy?"

The word of the Lord comes to us in the world in which we live and to which we are sent. To that word we say, "Yes, Lord!"

A Prayer

O God, the holy God, here we are in Your world. The house, the job, the room, the people, the things, the responsibilities. . . . (Would you stop praying now and visualize your world with your home, your family, your relationships?) *O Father, we say yes to our world. Don't let us think we can become more holy by leaving it. We know it is not Your will to take us out of it.*

Help us enter into our world by Your Spirit in a deeper way than ever before. We open our world to You. Break down every idol. Cast out every foe. We would be Your holy people— God-centered, Christlike, and sent to minister in the world where we live. Amen.

Chapter 12

"That was a terrible dinner. Let's have them over to our place for an even *worse* dinner!"

... Forgiving

by Robert Schuller

Background Scripture: Matthew 5:7; 6:14-15; Luke 23:34

WE ALL have our share of suffering. And we all have two choices when we face a terrible experience. We can choose the Be-Happy Attitude, or we can choose the Un-Happy Attitude.

The Un-Happy Attitude is the way of anger and vengeance. The Be-Happy Attitude is the way of mercy and forgiveness.

Jesus promised in the fifth beatitude: "Blessed are the merciful, for they shall obtain mercy" (Matthew 5:7, RSV). This beatitude holds three things—first, a *promise;* second, a *power principle* that has universal application; and third, a *prescription* for happy living.

The Promise

I first heard the following story 35 years ago. Years later, a variation appeared and was made famous by my friend, Tony Orlando, in his song, "Tie a Yellow Ribbon 'Round the Old Oak Tree." I have been told it's a true story, and I believe it, because I believe in the power of mercy.

Three teenagers boarded a bus in New Jersey. Seated on the bus was a quiet, poorly dressed man who sat alone and silent. When the bus made its first stop, everybody got off except this one man, who remained aloof and alone. When the kids came back on the bus, one of them said something nice to him, and he smiled shyly.

At the next bus stop, as everybody got off, the last teenager turned and said to the man, "Come on. Get off with us. At least stretch your legs."

So he got off. The teenagers invited him to have lunch with them. One of the young people said, "We are going to Florida for a weekend in the sun. It is nice in Florida, they say."

He said, "Yes, it is."

"Have you been there?"

"Oh, yes," he said, "I used to live there."

One said, "Well, do you still have a home and family?"

He hesitated. "I—I don't know," he said, finally.

"What do you mean, you don't know?" the teenager persisted.

Caught up by their warmth and their sincerity, he shared this story with them:

"Many years ago, I was sentenced to federal prison. I had a beautiful wife and wonderful children. I said to her,

'Honey, don't write to me. I won't write to you. The kids should not know that their dad is in prison. If you want to, go ahead and find another man—somebody who will be a good father to those boys.'

"I don't know if she kept her part of the bargain. I kept mine. Last week when I knew for sure I was getting out, I wrote a letter to our old address; it's just outside of Jacksonville. I said to her, 'If you are still living here and get this letter, if you haven't found anyone else, and if there is a chance of you taking me back—here is how you can let me know. I will be on the bus as it comes through town. I want you to take a piece of white cloth and hang it on the old oak tree right outside of town.'"

When they got back on the bus and they were about 10 miles from Jacksonville, all the teenagers moved to this man's side of the bus and pressed their faces against the windows. Just as they came to the outskirts of Jacksonville, there was the big oak tree. The teenagers let out a yell, and they jumped out of their seats. They hugged each other and danced in the center of the aisle. All they said was, "Look at it! Look at it!"

Not a single white cloth was tied to the tree. Instead there was a white bedsheet, a white dress, a little boy's white trousers, and white pillowcases! The whole tree was covered with dozens of pieces of white cloth!

That is the way God treats you and me. It is a promise from God that He will forget the past and erase the record we have rolled up. It is a promise that He will throw away the black pages of our book and give us the kind of big welcome that the prodigal son received from his father, who said, "My son that was lost is found and is home again" (Luke 15:24, my paraphrase). This is the *promise* of this beatitude.

Many people in my congregation would testify to the truth of God's promise in this beatitude. Their testimony is that when tragedy hits, they have found the capacity to find happiness anyway. Now, that's not human nature. The natural tendency would be to get angry, bitter, and cynical—to say, "There is no God." When a person reacts positively to tragedy—that's a miracle. Psalm 23 concludes with the glorious lines: "Surely goodness and mercy shall follow me all the days of my life" (RSV). That's God's way of saying that life will often be filled with goodness, but that even when God's goodness cannot be seen, His mercy can be experienced! In the midst of tears, heartbreak, enormous loss, and terrible sorrow, suddenly a sweet mood, like a gentle kiss, will touch your wounded heart. That experience is called mercy. It comes as an expression of God's love.

Throughout the Scriptures God promises that He will be merciful to us:

- "His *mercy* is on those who fear [trust] him" (Luke 1:50, RSV).

- "God, who is rich in *mercy*, out of the great love with which he loved us . . . made us alive together with Christ" (Ephesians 2:4-5, RSV).

The promise is there! It is for *you!* What wonderful news! What wonderful assurance! No matter where our road will lead, no matter what pain may hit, no matter what we do, God will be there with His mercy to forgive us, to hold us up, and carry us through the tough times. But this is only half of the beatitude: ". . . for they shall obtain mercy." The other half is, "Blessed are the merciful . . ."

What did Jesus mean when He said, "Blessed are the merciful, for they shall obtain mercy"?

I believe Jesus meant:

- God will be merciful to us.

- Then we will be merciful to others.

- Mercy will then come from a variety of sources.

The first step, then, is to accept God's mercy. All we need to do is *accept* the promise of the beatitude. It is God's promise that if we treat people mercifully, God will be merciful to us.

The Power Principle

The Bible also teaches a power principle that appears over and over again in the Bible, stated different ways:

- "If you do not forgive men their trespasses, neither will your Father forgive your trespasses" (Matthew 6:15, RSV).

- "The measure you give will be the measure you get" (Matthew 7:2, RSV).

Give a little, you get a little back. Give a lot, you get a lot back. This is the *law of proportionate return* that Jesus is teaching in these verses—and this beatitude. If you are critical, you can expect people to criticize you. If you refuse to forgive people, you can expect that these same people will refuse to forgive you. It is a law of life as real and unavoidable as the physical laws that control our world and our bodies.

Once, when I had laryngitis, I went to my throat doctor. The first thing he did was to get some gauze, wrap it around my tongue, pull my tongue out as far as he could, and stick a flat instrument far back in my throat. Inevitably, I gagged. He did it again. I gagged.

I said, "Done?"

To my dismay he said, "No, I have to do it again. I didn't get to see the vocal cords." Once more he prepared my tongue with another clean piece of gauze.

I said, "This time I'll practice positive thinking, and I won't gag."

He said, "Dr. Schuller, that won't work."

"Won't work?" I was appalled! That was the first time anybody had told me that possibility thinking wouldn't work.

The doctor quickly added, "Dr. Schuller, the gag is a reflex. Positive thinking cannot control reflexes, because reflexes come from the spinal cord. They don't pass through the brain."

Let me tell you something. In life there is a principle that you can compare with this biological reflex. If you act a certain way, you will get a certain response; there will be a guaranteed reflex action.

Here is a fundamental rule of life: If you want people to treat you nicely, treat them nicely. For every action, there is a reaction. For every positive action, there is a positive reaction. For every negative action, there is a negative reaction.

You can't tamper with natural laws. And this is a natural law: *If you treat people nicely, you will probably be treated nicely. The kinder you are to others, the more kindness you are likely to receive in life.*

The Prescription

The *prescription* for joyful living is very simple: If you want to be happy, treat people right.

I'll never forget the young wife who came to see me. She complained, "My husband never compliments me. All he does is criticize! It doesn't matter what I do, how hard I work; I only hear how I could have done it better!"

I suggested, "You know that people who are highly critical often suffer from a low self-esteem. Is it possible that your husband has trouble in that regard?"

She thought for a moment. "Yes, I think that's possible."

"Well," I replied, "then it seems to me that the way to help him with his self-esteem and his critical remarks is for you to start complimenting him!"

"Oh! I never thought of that!" she cried. "But you're right! I can't remember the last time I complimented him. I've been so busy looking for compliments *from* him that I've completely neglected compliments *for* him."

If you want to change your world, change yourself. How do you change yourself? How do you become this kind of positive-thinking person? I know only one way. Education does not do it. Legislation does not do it. However, there is a living God—and a living Christ—who does. Christ can come into hearts that are filled with fear, anger, bitterness, and hurt, and He can liberate them with His mercy. It can happon to you. It happens when you meet Jesus Christ and ask Him to take over your life.

Some of you have been the victims of racial or ethnic prejudice, or of some other form of painful discrimination such as sexism or ageism. You know the discomfort of being laughed at, ignored, not being allowed to fulfill your vocational dreams, just because you are a certain race, sex, or age.

Sometimes those people closest to us inflict the deepest, most painful wounds. Some of you would weep right now if I touched the tender memory, because of what a father or a mother, a spouse, child, lover, employer, or friend did to you.

Now the question is, *What do we do with these hidden wounds? How do we handle them?*

First of all, **don't nurse them.** There are many people who delight in nursing their hidden wounds. They still remember how their mother treated them. How their father treated them. How their first husband or first wife treated them. Thirty years later they are still obsessed with the wound. This is a neurotic, negative reaction.

Don't curse them. Don't let your wounds make you a bitter person. Don't allow anger at God or at the person who hurt you so deeply control your life. Don't curse your hurts, and **don't rehearse them.** Try to forget them. Remember, you can't forget your hurts if you keep talking about them *all the time.*

One of the great men on the staff of the church for 30 years here was a minister named Dr. Henry Poppen. Dr. Henry Poppen had been a missionary to China and was held prisoner for many months in a little town in China when the Communists took over. He was kept in solitary confinement, and the treatment he received was abysmal. The experience was tragic. It was horrific. It was awful. He escaped by miracle; most of the other missionaries were killed on sight. Well, when he came out, he was an emotionally wounded man. But he found healing for that wound through a doctor who said, "Don't talk about it anymore. Just forget it." In Dr. Poppen's case, these words of advice were just what he needed. His memories were so ugly that to have shared them over and over would have only made them that much more a part of his life.

Don't nurse the wound. Don't curse the wound. Don't keep rehearsing the wounding experience. What *do* you do with your hidden wounds? **Immerse them.** Drown them in the life of noble service.

I remember a time in the early years of my ministry when I had a real personal problem with someone. Sometimes it hurt me so badly I didn't know how to handle it. At these times my wife always had a solution. She'd say, "I think you should go out and call on Rosie Gray." Or "I think you ought to visit Marie; it was a year ago that her husband died."

So I would go out to the hospitals, and I would go calling on people. I would immerse myself as a pastor in the hearts of people who were hurting. And in the process, my little hidden wound was just drowned to death. It up and died.

How do you handle your hidden wounds? Don't nurse them. Don't curse them. Don't rehearse them. Do immerse them. And finally, **reverse them.** Turn the negative into a positive. You do that when you allow your wound to turn you into a more sensitive, compassionate, considerate, thoughtful, merciful, gracious person.

If your wound is something you can't share with others without criticizing somebody else or tearing him down, then you have to suffer in silence. If that's the case, then trust God. Let Him heal your hidden wounds.

She is no longer with us—our dear Schug. Her name was Bernice Schug, but my children called her simply "Schug." Since both my wife's and my families lived in the

Midwest, our children were unable to spend much time with their grandparents.

When we met Schug at church, she was a widow. Her own grandchildren lived in northern California, so she was unable to see them as often as she liked. It was inevitable then that Schug would become our California grandmother. She lavished love and poppy-seed rolls on us and our children. She stayed over with the children when my wife had our last two children. She ate meals with us, she cared for our children, yet none of us knew how deep her hidden wound was.

One day Schug came to me and said, "Bob, I was reading in the church bulletin today that you are having a guest speaker next Sunday. I see you're having a Kamikaze pilot as your guest."

Oh! I remembered then that Schug's son had been killed in World War II by a Kamikaze pilot. "That's right, Schug. This particular pilot was trained as a Kamikaze and would have died as a Kamikaze had the war not ended when it did. But he has a tremendous story to tell of how he found Jesus."

"That may be. I don't think I will be in church that Sunday, though. I don't think I could handle it."

"I understand," I replied. "I don't think it will hurt if you miss one Sunday."

The next Sunday the Japanese pilot told his story. His love and gratitude for Jesus shone from his black eyes. You could feel the love and release he had found.

People were moved by his testimony. And when the service was over, my associate pastor walked with him back down the aisle to the rear of the church.

Suddenly as they approached the last pew, an older woman stepped out. She stood firmly in front of the Kamikaze pilot and blocked his exit. She looked at him squarely and said, "My son was killed in the war by a Kamikaze!"

It was Schug. We all held our breath as she continued, "God has forgiven you for your sins, and tonight He has forgiven me of mine."

She threw her arms around this little Japanese pilot and hugged him and cried and cried as she released all the bitterness and anger that had been harbored for so many years.

Forgive a Kamikaze pilot, when a fellow pilot had killed a beloved son? Impossible! Yes, it is impossible for us, but not impossible for God!

After all, who is a better teacher on the subject of forgiveness than Jesus Christ? When He hung on the Cross, brutally whipped, mocked with a crown of thorns, betrayed by His friend, and deserted by His disciples, what did He say to the people who wanted Him to die?

He said, *"Forgive them;* for they know not what they do" (Luke 23:34, RSV).

If you are merciful, people will treat you mercifully. If you are merciful, then God will release you from vengeful attitudes that will eat at you and destroy you. When you follow the example that Christ set, you will find, much to your surprise, that God will step in and bless you, too, with an Easter morning!

From *The Be-Happy Attitudes,* by Robert Schuller, copyright 1985; used by permission of Word Books, Publisher, Waco, Tex.

Chapter 13

"Dear Lord, let me be the big cheese in the number-one job of the top outfit in the country, and let me come up with the right answers at the right times in the right places, but with it all, let me remain soft-spoken, country-shy, plain old Jeff Crotts from Spickard, Missouri."

... Happiness

by Gene Van Note

Background Scripture: Matthew 5:1-12

IT DIDN'T LOOK LIKE a place where you could buy happiness. In fact, it didn't look like much at all.

A corner lot. A collection of old cars—called "iron" by the used car salesman who catered to the poor, the underemployed, the welfare mother, and the alcoholic who had nearly reached bottom. Only he knew how much or how little his inventory was worth, for he lied to both the customer and the Internal Revenue Service with equal skill. But to the casual observer it didn't look like much.

And yet he was in the business of selling happiness.

If you could sit in the corner of his cluttered sales shack, as I did many times, you'd soon discover his predictable sales pitch.

After the customer had selected the car of his choice, presuming the salesman was able to get it started, the pitchman would ask, "Whadda ya hafta have?"

Translated, this meant, What is the most you can pay monthly to buy this slightly used, preowned, luxury vehicle?

If this did not move the car off the lot, the salesman would ask, "Whadd'l it take to make ya happy?"

That always amused me. The thought that a pile of "iron" could bring happiness. But the people who bought his cars really did seem to go away happy. He was, in fact, selling happiness. Or at least that form of pleasure that masquerades as happiness in our culture.

My private evaluation of life today supports the conclusion developed by professional pollsters. We are driven by the compulsion to be happy. We may not know what happiness is, where to find it, or how much it costs; but we are committed to own it or, at the very least, experience it. So it should not surprise us that our Lord had some specific things to say about happiness. However, as was so often the case, what Jesus taught was out of step with the spirit of the age, as foreign to His day as ours.

Happiness: A New Definition

Ex-presidents of the United States have the best job in the modern world, according to some observers. The Greeks of Christ's time were convinced their gods lived the ideal life. They had it all: money, power, prestige, sexual freedom to do as they pleased with whomever they pleased, and everything else needed to make life pleasurable. The word the Greeks used to describe the ultimate in well-being that the gods enjoyed was *makarios* (mah-CARE-e-os).

The Greeks believed that the best place to live in the ancient world was the island of Cyprus, which they called the Happy Isle. That title is one form of the word *makarios.* In their opinion, Cyprus had everything necessary for a life of unrestricted luxury. The climate was outstanding. Natural resources were abundant, containing all the minerals needed to make a person perfectly happy. The fields produced flowers, vegetables, and fruit to complete the idyllic scene.

The Greek concept of happiness, *makarios,* begins to come into focus. To be happy was to have every good thing, whenever you wanted it.

Then along came Jesus telling His disciples that the happy life, the life of greatest fulfillment, was *makarios* (Matthew 5:1-12 and a number of other places in the Gospels). But He used the word differently than it was being used by the Greeks of His generation. Marvin Vincent, in his book *Word Studies in the New Testament,* provides this concise definition of the word, as Christ used it. He says,

> Shaking itself loose from all thoughts of outward good, it *[makarios]* becomes the express symbol of happiness identified with pure character.

Most Bible versions use the word "blessed" to translate *makarios,* rather than the term "happy." But, literally, Jesus was saying, "You will be happy, as I define happiness, if you do these things."

Many times it is easier for us to understand a definition if we see it described. The word *box* is a good example. We know what a box is; we use one nearly every day. By definition, says Webster, a box is a rigid, typically rectangular receptacle often with a cover. It's hard to define, but we know one when we see it. That's why the next section is so important to our understanding of what Jesus said about happiness.

A Christian Description

Our Lord's foundational statement on happiness is known as the Beatitudes (Matthew 5:1-12). The first three beatitudes focus on our awareness of need. Then comes the great statement on how those needs can be satisfied. The final three describe the result of being satisfied.

First, awareness of need: the poor in spirit, those who mourn, and the meek (vv. 3-5). These are the folk who, because they recognize their spiritual bankruptcy, are engulfed with an overwhelming sadness that prompts them to turn to God for salvation.

"You can take a horse to water, but you can't make him drink," decrees the ancient proverb. To which my brother always added, "That's true; but you can put salt in his hay!" Like salt in the hay, an awareness of spiritual need develops a "hunger and thirst for righteousness" (v. 6). This desire will be abundantly filled.

"Blessed are the merciful . . . the pure in heart . . . the peacemakers" (vv. 7-9). These three beatitudes describe what happens when the seeker after Christ refuses to be content with anything less than God's answer for sin.

These people, says Christ, are the truly happy people. Happiness is what you are, not what you earn or what is given to you. Happiness is in the being, not the getting.

But there is more to Christian happiness.

One day Jesus did an unpredictable, and for most people, a humiliating thing. He washed the dirty feet of His fussing disciples (John 13:1-17). That got their attention.

He said, "I have set you an example that you should do as I have done for you" (v. 15). Then he concluded, "You will be blessed *[makarios]* if you do them" (v. 17).

Happiness is not only being but also doing. Doing what?

The dimensions of Christian happiness begin to take shape by looking at two related verses in the Gospel of Luke. In each one, the word Jesus uses, translated "blessed," is *makarios.*

"Blessed is she [Mary] who has believed that what the Lord has said to her will be accomplished" *(1:45).*

"Blessed is the mother who gave you birth" [a woman called out to Jesus] . . . He replied, "Blessed rather are those who hear the word of God and obey it" *(11:27-28).*

"If you want to be happy," Jesus said, "then obey My will for your life." It goes beyond the scope of this chapter to spell out God's will for us. Our purpose is to note that authentic happiness is selfless, not selfish.

"No one can get inner peace by pouncing on it, by vigorously willing to have it. Peace is a margin of power around our daily need," wrote American clergyman Harry Emerson Fosdick.

Peace is a dimension of power—Christ's power in us.

And so is happiness. Happiness is the result of an inner stability, not an outer security. It is not an accident. It does not drop out of the sky on "lucky" people. Perhaps that is why the Bible translators use the word blessed instead of happy. Happiness is a word that comes from the Old English word *hap*—a force that shapes events unpredictably: chance, luck, fortune.

This is not a haphazard world. On the contrary, it is a fundamentally dependable, entirely predictable world, where peaches grow on peach trees, not on watermelon vines. The tendency of humans is to search for happiness outside themselves. The frantic pursuit of things to do, places to go, and stuff to swallow has a price tag amounting to billions of dollars each year.

"Here is the psychological soundness of the Christian teaching on conversion," says preacher J. Wallace Hamilton. "When the total self is awakened, when the whole being comes alive unto God and begins to move somewhere unanimously, God puts the sound of laughter in the soul."

But there is more to doing than just a self-improvement program. We are to do for others.

Listen again to the words of Luke: "When you give a banquet, invite the poor, the crippled, the lame, the blind, and you will be blessed" (14:13-14).

Dr. Geneva Hall and her three children looked forward to Christmas with despair. Her husband, their father, had just died. In a family conference they decided on a way to honor both his memory and the Christ of Christmas. Each person made a list of what they wanted, putting the most desired gift at the top. The agreement was that this item would not be purchased. Instead the money would be pooled to buy dolls for girls at a nearby children's home. On Christmas morning, before they opened their own gifts, they drove over to the home and gave the gifts to the little girls. This act of unselfishness brought so much joy it became a holiday tradition in their home.

Christian happiness is a by-product of unselfishness.

The Challenge We Face

The United States of America was begun with a Declaration of Independence. In this declaration, the founders of a new nation declared that all people have been endowed by their Creator with certain inalienable rights. Among them, the right to pursue happiness. The sons and daughters of those early leaders are putting that "right" into practice with unbridled fury. Americans have been on the move seeking the good life: east to west, house to house, job to job, marriage to marriage. Nothing is allowed to stand in the way of the "pursuit of happiness."

We live in a breathless generation on a futile pursuit, like greyhounds chasing the mechanical rabbit at the dog racing tracks. Once in a while, someone will pause in this wild pursuit for a few quiet moments. The renewal that quietness brings is so dramatic, some presume they have found real peace. National columnist Erma Bombeck observed out loud, "I wonder if happiness is something wild, and gets skittish when pursued. Perhaps it comes to people most easily when they're still, or hold out their lives quietly like an open hand."

This bumper sticker I've seen comes close to expressing our culture's attitude toward happiness: "The One Who Dies with the Most Toys—WINS!" But neither quietness nor the toys of life bring true pleasure.

What did Jesus say about happiness? It's OK to be happy, He said.

Then He added that we will find it only in Him as we serve others.

Revolutionary? Without a doubt. But it works.

Gene Van Note is executive editor of Adult Ministries at the Church of the Nazarene Headquarters, Kansas City.

Other Dialog Series Books

Building Self-esteem
The Christian and Money Management
Christian Personality Under Construction
Christians at Work in a Hurting World
Christians in a Crooked World
Coping with Traumas of Family Life
Finding My Place
Happiness Is Growing a Marriage
How to Improve Your Prayer Life
How to Live the Holy Life
Life Issues . . . That Can't Be Ignored
No Easy Answers
Questions You Shouldn't Ask About
    Christianity
Questions You Shouldn't Ask About the Church
Single Again: Survival Kit for the Divorced
    and Widowed
Timeless Truths for Timely Living
Tough Questions—Christian Answers
When Life Gets Rough

For a description of all available Dialog Series books,
including some that may not be listed here,
contact your local bookstore or your publishing house
and ask for the free Dialog Series brochure.